AMÉLIE VINCENT
Signature Dishes.

50 chefs share their secret recipes

Lannoo

8   **Intro** – Amélie Vincent

10   Massimiliano Alajmo (LE CALANDRE)
Saffron risotto with liquorice powder.

14   Josean Alija (NERUA GUGGENHEIM)
Kokotxas and white asparagus omelette.

20   Juan Mari & Elena Arzak (ARZAK)
Marbled egg – egg, zizania and mushroom marbling.

24   Garima Arora (GAA)
Chaat.

28   Maksut Aşkar (NEOLOKAL)
'Kadınbudu' meatballs.

34   Eneko Atxa (AZURMENDI)
Teardrop peas and Iberian gel.

42   José Avillez (BELCANTO)
A Dip in the Sea.

48   Ivan & Sergey Berezutsky (FORMERLY TWINS GARDEN)
Armavir. (3D-printed potato flower with smoked lard butterfly)

52   Massimo Bottura (OSTERIA FRANCESCANA)
Five ages of Parmigiano Reggiano in different textures and at different temperatures.

56   Manu Buffara (MANU)
Cauliflower, passionfruit and peanuts.

62   Riccardo Camanini (LIDO 84)
Cacio e pepe pasta en vessie.

66   Mateu Casañas, Oriol Castro & Eduard Xatruch (DISFRUTAR)
Panchino filled with caviar and sour cream.

70   Vicky Cheng (VEA)
Roasted sea cucumber.

74 Andre Chiang (RAW AND SICHUAN MOON)
'Memory 1997': foie gras, truffle, chive.

78 Paul Chung (SAISON HOSPITALITY)
California Urchin Gimmari.

82 Mauro Colagreco (MIRAZUR)
Beetroot caviar.

88 Alexandre Couillon (LA MARINE)
Oysters with lardo and squid bouillon.

92 Sang Hoon Degeimbre (L'AIR DU TEMPS)
Les Jardins de Liernu.

98 Richard Ekkebus (AMBER)
Aka Uni cauliflower, lobster and Daurenki Tsar Impérial caviar.

102 Adeline Grattard (YAM'TCHA)
Island octopus.

106 Mehmet Gürs (MIKLA)
Balık ekmek. (fried hamsi sandwich)

110 Brian Mark Hansen (SØLLERØD KRO)
Lemon sole with fermented daikon sauce, parsley and Ossetra caviar.

114 Zaiyu Hasegawa (DEN)
DFC. (Den fried chicken)

118 Sergio Herman (LE PRISTINE)
Mussels with marinera sauce.

122 Willem Hiele (WILLEM HIELE RESTAURANT)
Shrimp bisque.

126 Dan Hunter (BRAE)
Parsnip and apple.

130 Supaksorn 'Ice' Jongsiri (SORN)
'The sea holds the forest.'

134 Hiroyasu Kawate (FLORILÈGE)
Sustainability beef.

138 Santiago Lastra (KOL)
Langoustine tacos.

144 Corey Lee (BENU)
Thousand-year-old quail's eggs with potage and preserved ginger.

148 Ángel León (APONIENTE)
Sea salad.

152 Richie Lin (MUME)
MUME salad.

158 Virgilio Martínez (CENTRAL)
Amazonian fish and tucupi.

164 Dabiz Muñoz (DIVERXO)
The Ages of Hake.

170 Nicolai Nørregaard (KADEAU BORNHOLM)
Raw queen scallop, 'mussel liquorice', horseradish cream, chewy tomatoes and blackcurrant wood oil.

176 Junghyun Park (ATOBOY)
Atoboy fried chicken.

182 Christophe Pelé (LE CLARENCE)
Turbot collar with XO sauce.

186 Edoardo Pellicano (FORMERLY MAOS)
Marco Polo noodles.

190 Dave Pynt (BURNT ENDS)
Western Australian marron with tobiko and kombu beurre blanc.

194 Emmanuel Renaut (FLOCONS DE SEL)
Wild mushrooms with a baked cheese crust.

198 Joan Roca (EL CELLER DE CAN ROCA)
Soil and oyster.

202 João Rodrigues (MATÉRIA)
Squid with sheep's butter and chives.

206 Julien Royer (ODETTE)
Kampot pepper – crusted pigeon.

212 Ana Roš (HIŠA FRANKO)
Where is the meat?

218 Prateek Sadhu (FORMERLY MASQUE)
Unicorn Pani Puri.

222 Eyal Shani (HASALON)
The original world-famous baby cauliflower.

226 Kwok Keung Tung (THE CHAIRMAN)
Steamed flower crab with Shaoxing rice wine and chicken fat.

230 Aaron Turner (IGNI)
Fermented Dutch potatoes poached in goat milk and single-press olive oil with smoked dried brook trout roe.

234 Jorge Vallejo (QUINTONIL)
Charred avocado tartare with escamoles and Mexican herb chips.

240 Poul Andrias Ziska (KOKS)
Ræstan fisk and garnatálg.

246 **Weights & liquid measures table**

247 **Photocredits**

—— THE SIGNATURE DISH. A dish that symbolises in just a few mouthfuls the identity of its creator. A dish behind which hides a search, a meaning, an encounter. A dish that lays out a bit of history or a culinary philosophy on a beautifully presented plate, and that leaves us guessing until we are told its unique origin story. A dish with multiple colours, textures and flavours that honours nature and takes us on a journey to discover the inner, secret world of the chef.

My name is Amélie Vincent and I am very lucky to work in the world of gastronomy with the most creative chefs in the world. Almost ten years ago I became an official tastehunter and content creator for the World's 50 Best, the platform that lists the best restaurants in the world. Today, I am also a TV host, consultant, journalist, and influencer.

I didn't find my vocation by chance. As my dad once said, 'it was guided by life, its mountains and its valleys'. As an only child, from a mixed European and Asian background, and with globetrotting parents eager to make new discoveries, I've had plenty of opportunities to soak up and discover diverse cultures. I remember at barely three years old being the youngest gourmet to sit at the table at Georges Blanc – three Michelin stars at the time.

Later, I visited the pagodas where my family went to pray to our ancestors, tasting the delicious dumplings made by the monks, and travelled to African villages where I discovered how to crush cassava. I followed my father to remote islands, and stepped into the roadside huts, while he was saying: 'Choose a dish on the menu with your eyes closed, it will surely tell us something.'

So I have always bathed in this melting pot of culinary curiosity and cultural discovery. At those different tables, I dissected the flavours of course, but I also observed with great interest these animated human beings who tirelessly repeated the same gestures to feed us. The profession of chef fascinated me very early on; as a child I was in awe of the magic of the ingredients' transformation in the kitchen, and the joy of sharing at the dinner table.

This sense of wonder for all things culinary never left me, and eventually led me to change my job as an intellectual property lawyer for the world of gastronomy. Then I discovered the work of the most creative chefs in the world, such as Virgilio Martínez and his wife Pia León and their Mater Iniciativa project, which promotes Peru's culinary heritage and biodiversity, or chef Mehmet Gürs and anthropologist Tangor Tan, who have been searching all year long the most historic foods in Turkey to express the essence of their country.

I am grateful to have had the opportunity to meet dozens of talented chefs, who took the time to present their terroirs to me, tell me all about their sources of inspiration, and revealed the magic of nature and of human beings hidden behind their choice of ingredients or cooking techniques.

Then, on a more personal note, when faced with the adversity of life, it is these same chefs – who had by then become friends – who took care to feed me wonderful dishes, to give me back the courage to continue on my journey.

Therefore, this book is more than a collection of individual recipes. It is a tribute to my soul family, and a look back at the ten years I spent travelling the world, fascinated by the life force and passion that drives all these chefs to create so many ephemeral masterpieces. which disappear as quickly as their beauty touches us.

I would like to thank this amazing family of chefs from all over the world (who unfortunately could not all be present in this first edition) for letting me open the door to their kitchens, and invite me to join their tables and personal lives. I humbly hope this book will open another small door... One that will reveal to readers a part of the beauty and subtlety that I had the chance to experience, touch and taste along this unique initiatic journey.
Because in life, as in the kitchen, transmission is key.

To my mother, this esthete who left too soon and taught me about beauty and taste,
To my children, who share this fascination and curiosity
To my soul family: my dear friends in the industry,
To the passion that allows us to reveal the best of ourselves,
To love, nature, and the beauty of creativity,

AMÉLIE VINCENT
The Foodalist Studio
@thefoodalist

Massimiliano Alajmo.

LE CALANDRE, PADUA (IT)

Born in Padua in 1974, Massimiliano Alajmo was born into a long line of chefs and restaurateurs. After attending a management school, Massimiliano was culinary educated in the kitchen of Alfredo Chiocchetti of Ja Navalge in Moena, Marc Veyrat of Aberge de l'Eridan in Veyrier-du-Lac and Les Près d'Eugénie in Eugénie-les-Bains. The chef took over his family's restaurant when he was just 19, and at age 28 he became the youngest three-star Michelin chef in history.

—— Family is key to Alajmo, who grew up in his parents' restaurant in Rubano, in Italy's Veneto region, and later took it over with his equally talented brother Raffaele, a sommelier. No wonder his signature dish, saffron risotto, is dedicated to his wife Maria Pia and her home region of Calabria.

'The root and the flower, represented by liquorice and saffron, are the most extreme parts of the plant; one low, deep and hidden, the other tall, seductive and luminous, almost like a dialogue between opposites: origin and growth, birth and rebirth,' explains Alajmo, who is also known as *Il Mozart dei Fornelli* (The Mozart of the stoves) for the lightness, depth of flavour and fluidity of his cuisine. According to Alajmo, 'the colours of the risotto reflect the contrast, at the same time maintaining a hidden truth, while the dark powder manifests golden reflections only in the presence of light.'

The sunshine-coloured risotto is usually served as a first course in a tasting menu (with other classics such as cuttlefish cappuccino, scorched bone marrow with sea urchin, and almond mozzarella), but has also been served in different variations over the years, including a risotto 'Passi d'Oro' inspired by Roberto Barni's sculpture at the Uffizi gallery. It is best enjoyed sitting at one of Le Calandre's wooden tables, sculpted from 300-year-old trees, but if you decide to make it yourself and can't find liquorice powder, Alajmo suggests replacing it with a few drops of blood orange reduction, orange zest and chopped parsley.

The Alajmo empire currently includes a bistro and a deli in Rubano, as well as many establishments in Venice, from St Mark's Square to La Certosa island, and stretches far beyond the Venetian shores, with Sesamo in Marrakesh and Caffè Stern in Paris. You can also purchase the perfect riso carnaroli and olive oil from Alajmo's online boutique. *Ingredienti* are the crux of Alajmo's cooking. As he once said: 'There is no truth beyond that contained in the ingredients. My goal is to reach or penetrate the essence of the ingredient, and respond with respect and therefore lightness.'

MASSIMILIANO ALAJMO - LE CALANDRE

Saffron risotto with liquorice powder.

SERVES 4

FOR THE SAFFRON REDUCTION

50g water, boiled
2g saffron powder

Dissolve the saffron in the boiling water.

FOR THE RISOTTO

320g Carnaroli rice
12g extra-virgin olive oil
70g dry white wine
a pinch of salt
1g saffron threads
30g saffron reduction
2L chicken broth
60g butter
80g grated Parmigiano Reggiano
5g fresh lemon juice
2g dark liquorice powder
a pinch of caster sugar

Toast the rice in a wide saucepan with the olive oil. Add the wine and allow to evaporate. Add the pinch of salt and saffron threads, then continue cooking, adding first 30g of the saffron reduction and then the broth, a ladle at a time. Once cooked, remove from the heat and briskly stir in the butter, Parmigiano Reggiano and lemon juice. Emulsify with a little broth.

TO PLATE

Ladle onto a flat plate, allowing the risotto to spread. Sprinkle with the liquorice powder and garnish with a few drops and brush strokes of the saffron reduction.

Josean Alija.

NERUA GUGGENHEIM, BILBAO (ES)

Born in 1978 in the Basque Country, Josean Alija began his training at age 14. In 2011, the chef launched Nerua, now a Michelin-starred restaurant, at the famed Guggenheim Museum Bilbao.

— Alija always knew he wanted to be a chef, but before he eventually began working at the Guggenheim Museum Bilbao, his career wasn't all plain sailing. In fact it came to a stop in 1998, when a motorcycle accident left him in a coma for 21 days, after which he awoke to find that he had lost his sense of taste and smell and had to learn to regain them. So it's probably no coincidence that his cooking is about pursuing pure flavours and assembling them in harmony, a philosophy he calls 'Muina', or essence.

Alija's menu at Nerua follows the pace of the seasons, and his creations are rooted in the vegetable gardens and farms of the Basque Country and the plentiful catch of the day from the Bay of Biscay. His signature dish is a simple omelette, accompanied by a different product (such as courgette or white asparagus), depending on the season, and featuring the local fish stew kokotxas. 'It is inspired by chef Sacha Hormaechea's "Lazy Omelette"', explains Alija. 'It's based on the concept of sharing and coming together to enjoy. It talks about my informal, rogue and fun side that invites you to have a good time and enjoy good food.'

Simplicity is the name of the game here. Alija's dishes are pared back, with very few products, taste and textures. Yet his omelette is, of course, much more than an omelette: a base of curdled egg filled with spicy oyster mayonnaise, egg sabayon and grilled hake kokotxas.
'Our cooking is based on the defence of products, nature and essence,' explains the chef. 'We mostly work with seasonal products, using vegetables as one of our main ingredients. Flavour is as important as texture and naturalism in the assembly of the dishes, and creativity and technique are the base that exalts the products we use.'

Working in one of the world's most iconic art museums also brings its own visual influence: Alija's dishes are perfect abstract compositions with flashes of colour brought by the freshest ingredients possible. Only he can serve an omelette that looks like a masterpiece.

JOSEAN ALIJA - NERUA GUGGENHEIM

Kokotxas and white asparagus omelette.

SERVES 4

FOR THE WHITE ASPARAGUS

200g white asparagus

Peel and slice the asparagus, then boil in plenty of salted water for 15 minutes. Stop further cooking by plunging into a reverse bain-marie. Reserve the asparagus cooking water for the sabayon.

FOR THE EGG YOLK AND ASPARAGUS SABAYON

160g free-range egg yolks
60ml of the asparagus cooking water
0.9g xanthan gum (6g per litre of juice)
fine salt

Texturise the asparagus cooking water with the xanthan gum. Place the texturised water and the egg yolks in a bowl, and boil in a bain-marie until the mixture reaches 63 °C (145 °F), stirring constantly. Once the temperature is reached, blend and strain the sabayon. Add salt and place in a syphon with 3 gas charges. Keep refrigerated until use.

FOR THE LEEK AND OYSTER EMULSION

35g leek juice
30g fresh and cleaned oyster
2g lemon juice
70g sunflower oil
0.1g xanthan gum
fine salt

Mix the oyster with the leek juice and the xanthan gum in a blender for 2 minutes. Add the olive oil slowly, emulsifying the mixture like a mayonnaise. Once all the oil is fully integrated, add the lemon juice. Add salt if necessary and keep refrigerated.

FOR THE OMELETTE

2 eggs
2 egg yolks
fine salt

Mix the whole eggs with the yolks, season with salt and cook as if it were a crepe in a 26cm-diameter non-stick frying pan.

FOR THE BRINED SEAWEED

1000g water
30g fine salt
35g seaweed

Mix all the ingredients in a container and blend. Strain them using a Superbag (a special strainer) and keep refrigerated until use.

FOR THE BILBAÍNA OIL

250g olive oil
13g sliced garlic cloves, removing the germ
½ small cayenne pepper

Mix all the ingredients together cold and set over a heat. Once the garlic starts turning golden, remove from the heat and let it cool down. Strain and keep refrigerated until use.

FOR THE CANDIED AND SMOKED KOKOTXAS

30 units big hake kokotxas
250g bilbaína oil

Place the kokotxas into the sea lettuce brine for 10 minutes, then dry well and set aside. Heat the bilbaína oil in a saucepan until it reaches 65 °C (149 °F) and add the kokotxas for about 2 minutes, taking care not to break the skins. Once confited, remove the kokotxas and smoke them on the grill.

TO FINISH AND PLATE

chervil leaves

Have the syphon of the sabayon heated beforehand (minimum 5 minutes) in the Roner at 70 °C (160 °F). Heat the kokotxa in the salamander grill. Place the omelette curdled on one side only, as an 'open omelette'. Spread the oyster emulsion over the omelette, then cover with hot asparagus sabayon. Heat the hake kokotxas in the salamander grill for 20 seconds and place them on the top. Brush with spicy bilbaína oil.
Finish with the asparagus slices and some chervil leaves.

Juan Mari & Elena Arzak.

ARZAK, BILBAO (ES)

Born in 1942, Juan Mari Arzak is considered one of the great masters of New Basque cuisine. The chef works with his daughter Elena in their award-winning restaurant, originally founded in 1897 by his grandparents.

—— There's no need to introduce Juan Mari Arzak to any self-respecting, fine-dining aficionado. The San Sebastian native has made Basque cuisine one of the most innovative and respected cuisines in the world, while his restaurant has been awarded no less than three Michelin stars since 1989. Since the 1990s, Juan Mari has been working in tandem with his daughter Elena, winner of the 2012 Veuve Clicquot World's Best Female Chef Award, described by no other than the former head chef of elBulli Ferran Adrià, 'as one of the most important chefs in history'.

'This dish is part of our history. This is our story,' says Elena. 'The egg is always a fresh egg, laid that morning. We get them thanks to the invaluable support of our farmers. The egg was a great luxury for my father when he was young because his mother was from a traditional Basque farmhouse and they used to sell all the fresh eggs they had.' From these humble roots comes a superlative dish, the marbled egg. 'It elevates a simple product,' she says. 'It's cooked at a low temperature using a technique which creates a marbled effect, contrasting with the zizania which is the seed of a plant, and it's seasoned with millenary egg and a bit of grated lime zest.'

This signature dish joins a long list of eggy delicacies at Arzak, where there is always an egg dish on the tasting menu. Past creations include a graffiti-inspired egg decorated with green parsley sauce and squid ink sauce, or the ever-popular Arzak poached egg, while Juan Mari's own all-time favourite is scrambled eggs with piquillo peppers.

Like all of the restaurant's creations, the marble egg was planned and prepared in the chef's lab, where creativity, ingenuity and inspiration wander freely about. Here, the Arzaks and their team test flavours and textures, and define new concepts to integrate into the ever-changing menu. At their disposal is cutting-edge culinary technology, and a flavour workbench with more than a thousand products and ingredients, all neatly labelled in perfectly lined-up containers. As Elena once stated: 'Our food always tastes of now: we use the latest technologies and scientific techniques to evolve.'

JUAN MARI & ELENA ARZAK - ARZAK

Marbled egg – egg, zizania and mushroom marbling.

SERVES 4

FOR THE MUSHROOM PRALINE*

500g dehydrated wild mushrooms
750g sunflower oil
10g salt

Chop the dehydrated mushrooms and push through a sieve. Add the oil to a wet grinder and gradually add the mushroom powder. Allow to refine for 1 hour at minimum pressure and then for 10 hours at maximum pressure. Reserve.

FOR THE MUSHROOM 'PRALINE CREAM'

50g mushroom praline
500g milk
5g soy sauce

Mix the mushroom praline together with the milk and soy sauce. Using a whisk, mix vigorously until well blended and creamy. Reserve.

FOR THE EGGS

6g mushroom 'praline cream'
4 eggs, freshly laid that day
zest of 1 lime
salt and pepper

Use the mushroom 'praline cream' to paint 4 sheets of cling film with horizontal stripes. Place an egg on each of the cling film sheets, wrap, and tie closed with a knot. Reserve.

FOR THE GOOSE LIVER MOUSSE

60g sautéed goose liver
35g cream
salt and pepper

Sauté the goose liver and drain. Blend together with the cream until the mixture is smooth. Season with salt and pepper.

* These are the exact quantities to achieve the desired result in the wet grinder.

FOR THE ZIZANIA

30g zizania (wild rice)
100ml olive oil
1 pinch of salt

Heat the oil and fry the zizania until soft. Drain well and season.

TO PLATE

Boil the water and cook the eggs in the cling film for 4 minutes. Once the time is up, very carefully remove the cling film. Set the eggs aside.
Place a teaspoon of the mushroom 'praline cream' and another of the goose liver mousse in the middle of a wide, shallow bowl. Arrange an egg on top. Place a few pieces of the century egg white next to it. Grate a little lime zest over the whole dish.
Finally, arrange the fried zizania around the egg.

Garima Arora.

GAA, BANGKOK (TH)

The first Indian woman to win a Michelin star in 2018, Garima Arora hails from Mumbai. The chef studied in Paris and worked at Noma before heading to Thailand in 2017 to work for Gaggan Anand. It was there that she opened Gaa, receiving instant acclaim.

— 'To me, chaat is the perfect introduction to the flavours of India,' explains Arora, who grew up in a typical Punjabi food-loving household. Inspired by this fried dough served on the streets in India, the chef says: Part of the experience of eating chaat is savouring the flavour combination and discovering the ingredients as you go along. Our take on chaat has frozen pomegranate in the centre and all the other ingredients are hidden underneath. You will have to dig in and get everything in the bottom to discover the rest.' This sense of discovery and wonder is central to Arora's approach: 'Cooking should have an element of surprise. I chase after that feeling of having something new for the very first time.'

Her chaat comes beautifully served on a simple wooden spoon at Gaa, situated in a traditional Thai house in the heart of Bangkok, where she shares her passion for India's myriad culinary specialities and serves dishes including unripe jackfruit with roti and pickles, and a chocolate-covered betel leaf. Although her favourite ingredients are the easily sourced lime, black salt and fresh fruits, Arora also works with small farmers and foraging tribes to add some more unique delicacies to her menu.

Arora explains where her passion for food come from: 'My father has been most influential in my career as a chef. He was the first to teach me how to cook, instiling in me a love for cooking from an early age. My earliest and fondest memory is of cooking with my father when I was young. I think it's because he never treated cooking like a chore. He always approached it with joy, passion and curiosity.

Today Arora is on a mission to transform the narrative on Indian food, which she feels is often misrepresented due to a skewed focus on the country's imperial past. The chef is doing this both through her cooking at Gaa and through the non-profit initiative she founded in 2019 called Food Forward India, a unique, travelling initiative that aims to map India's varied rural, tribal and urban cuisines and share them around the world.

GARIMA ARORA - GAA

Chaat.

SERVES 6 – 7

FOR THE SWEET YOGHURT

125g strained yoghurt or Greek yoghurt
20g icing sugar
1g ground cardamom

Mix the hung yoghurt or Greek yoghurt with the icing sugar and cardamom powder. Set aside to rest in the refrigerator.

FOR THE POMEGRANATE GLAZE

500ml pomegranate juice

Reduce the pomegranate juice over a medium heat until syrupy.

FOR THE FROZEN POMEGRANATE

1 pomegranate, deseeded
115g frozen strawberries
170ml pomegranate juice
black salt, to taste
cumin powder, to taste
chilli powder, to taste
salt, to taste
lime juice, to taste
1 sheet gelatine

Blend the frozen strawberries with 170ml of pomegranate juice and reduce over a medium heat until reduced by around 25 %.
Let the liquid cool down, then season with the chaat masala, black salt, cumin powder, chilli powder, salt and lime. The flavour should be sour, salty and sweet.
Warm the liquid, then add the gelatine sheet and let it dissolve. Add to a round, thin mould to create a disc and store in the freezer until frozen.

FOR THE LEMON BASIL CHUTNEY

25g lemon basil leaves

Blanch the lemon basil leaves, then blend with 63g water and a pinch of salt.

FOR THE CRISPY BETEL AND
MANGO LEAVES

50g betel leaf, thinly sliced
50g mango leaf, thinly sliced
neutral oil for frying

Fry finely sliced betel and mango leaves in neutral oil until crispy and salt to taste.

FOR THE SEV SEASONING
(TO MAKE 100G)

TO PLATE

100g sev, crispy chickpea snack
black salt, to taste
cumin, to taste
chilli powder, to taste
chaat masala, to taste

Brush the frozen pomegranate disc thinly with the pomegranate glaze. In a bowl, first plate the sweet yoghurt, pomegranate seeds, lemon basil chutney and sev, then place the frozen pomegranate on top. Garnish with the fried betel and mango leaves.

Maksut Aşkar.

NEOLOKAL, ISTANBUL (TR)

The chef-owner of Neolokal, Maksut Aşkar, celebrates Anatolian cuisine inspired by his childhood memories and traditions at his Michelin-starred restaurant, perfectly located in Istanbul's Salt Galata Museum.

— Originally from south-eastern Turkey, Aşkar is keen to celebrate and explore all the different culinary facets of his native region. 'My hometown borders Syria and was under French influence for 30 years, so my family's cuisine is Levantine cuisine,' he explains. 'Yet Anatolia is a majority of minorities, a vast richness of culinary heritage. I am seeking ways to melt all those cultures in one pot. Inspired by the food of the mothers of Anatolia, I describe my cuisine as an honest reflection of our humble food culture.'

This wealth of gastronomic specialities made choosing a signature dish a tricky task. 'We try to gather as many of our favourites from our traditions, childhood memories and the very rich food culture of Anatolia,' says Aşkar who in the end settled for kadınbudu, an oval meatball named after the shape of a woman's thigh. 'This dish is mainly served at the *esnaf lokantası* (tradesmen's restaurants), where it's traditionally served with mashed or fried potatoes.' Aşkar's version might contain both meatball and potatoes, but it looks completely different than the hearty dish it is inspired by.

It's all part of Aşkar's plan to bring different stories and interplays to the dining table: 'I believe we need to find ways to create interaction between ourselves, the food and the people with whom we are sharing the food. We are the bridge between the stories, the food, the culture, the childhood memories and the guests. By using new ways of thinking and combining modern technology with traditional techniques, we try to update our traditional recipes, so that they can be accepted in the future.'

Aşkar still feels there is much more to discover in Anatolia, especially in terms of different techniques and ingredients used in the region's kitchens. 'I am seeking ways to harmonise all of them in one kitchen,' he says. 'I have many favourite ingredients for different seasons and parts of Anatolia. I like to cook recipes with stories that make me smile.'

MAKSUT AŞKAR - NEOLOKAL

'Kadınbudu' meatballs.

SERVES 10

FOR THE MEATBALLS
MAKES 30

1500g chicken mince
100g smoked beef fat
8g cumin
150g boiled rice
2 eggs
20g parsley
15g mint
15g flour
100g breadcrumbs
100g onion

Pass the boneless chicken pieces and smoked beef fat through the meat grinder. Cut the onions *en brunoise* and lightly sauté in a pan, then add the chicken mince and spices and cook whisking all the while. Set aside to cool. After the mixture has cooled, add the eggs, parsley, breadcrumbs, mint, chicken broth and cooked rice. Put the mixture in a square mould.

FOR THE POTATO CRISPS
MAKES 32 CRISPS

4 baking potatoes

Cut the potatoes into 1.5mm slices on a mandoline, turn them into rounds using a cutter, then soak in cold water. Reserve the potato trimmings. Cut out 2 rectangles of greaseproof paper that will fit between 2 1/1 Teflon trays. Brush one tray with oil and cover with one of the greaseproof paper rectangles.
Put the potatoes in plenty of salted water and soften for a maximum of 4 minutes. Wash the potato slices in cold water, then remove the excess water with a napkin, and place the potato slices on the greaseproof paper on the tray. (The tray should take 32 pieces, set 4 by 8). After placing the potatoes between 2 greased wax papers, put the wax papers filled with potatoes between two trays and put them in the oven.
Bake at 150 °C (300 °F) full fan for 8 minutes, and then at 180 °C (355 °F) at level 3 for a further 7 minutes. If all or some of the potato crisps are not yet golden brown, bake for a further 2–3 minutes.

FOR THE CHICKEN FOAM
MAKES ENOUGH FOR 1 SYPHON
(40 PORTIONS)

450g potato trimmings
750g chicken broth
20ml apple cider vinegar
16g salt
400g cream
400g chicken thigh meat

Cook all the ingredients except the cream in the chicken broth until the potatoes melt into the mixture. Add the cream and boil for 1–2 minutes. Remove the mixture from the stove, blend in a Thermomix, and then pass through a strainer. Syphon and squeeze 3 chargers. Keep at 70 °C (160 °F) sous vide until service.

FOR THE CONFIT LEMONS

500g lemon juice
1kg lemon peel from the squeezed lemons
250g sugar

Use the squeezed leftover lemons and blanch the lemon peel 10 times. Mix the lemon juice and sugar with a hand blender. Put in vacuum bags and bake at 60 °C (140 °F) for 3 hours.

FOR THE CONFIT LEMON JAM

300g confit lemon
600g sugar
600g of water

Remove the white layers of the confit lemons, so that only the yellow peel remains, and then cut into strings.
Put on the stove with the sugar and water, and boil until thick and jam-like.

FOR THE CRISPY CHICKEN
SKIN

3 whole chicken skins

Remove the excess fat by scraping the chicken skins with the help of a spatula. Roll the skins between 2 layers of greaseproof paper and put it in a 200 °C (390 °F) oven between 2 trays for 30 minutes.

FOR THE CHICKEN DEMI-GLACE
MAKES 40 PORTIONS

1kg red onions
450g carrots
325g celery stalks
325g leek
500g red pepper
2 bottles of red wine
200g tomato paste
8kg chicken wings plus chicken bones if available
50 garlic cloves
5 bay leaves
100ml sunflower oil
20L iced water

Cut the vegetables, except the red onions, in mirepoix and sear in a pan with the sunflower oil. Peel the red onions, cut in half, and sear on the plate. Bake the chicken bones smeared with the tomato paste at 250 °C (480 °F) for 25 minutes.
Put all the ingredients into a pot with the iced water. Simmer for 24 hours, filter the stock and separate the stock from the excess fat.

FOR THE MEATBALLS

eggs
flour
squares

Whisk the eggs until smooth. Dip the squares into flour and cover with the eggs. Fry until golden crisp.

TO FINISH AND PLATE
FOR EACH PORTION

Add the ingredients below to the plate as to your preference:
3 fried chicken squares
45g potato mousse
12g chicken demiglace
3g confit lemon
3g chicken chips
3g potato chips
A dust of 0.1g coriander powder

Eneko Atxa.

AZURMENDI, LARRABETZU (ES)

Born in 1973, Eneko Atxa is a three Michelin-starred chef whose flagship restaurant, Azurmendi in the region of Biscay, attracts gourmets from all corners of the world. With a strong focus on sustainability, Basque traditions and its local environment, Atxa offers a culinary experience, dedicated to the conservation of endemic species, dividing it into different stages that take place across the entire restaurant building.

× **What does your signature dish tell us about you?**

ENEKO ATXA: *Tear pea and Iberian gel. It's one of our customers' favourite dishes; there are those who come in the spring season especially for it. It talks about our land, our products and producers; four well-defined seasons with different products; our culture, our Basque culinary heritage and our way of understanding gastronomy.*

× **What is the story behind its creation?**

ENEKO ATXA: *Tear pea is a very rare product. Produced a few days only during the spring season, it is extremely fragile: producers and chefs need to be careful while they are working on it, taking every grain by hand, without breaking it.*

I like its preciousness and its texture that reminds me of a sea roe, exploding in your mouth. Each burst of it has an authentic vegetal hit, with a sweet shade.

× **How would you describe your cooking and the philosophy behind it?**

ENEKO ATXA: *A cuisine that emanates from a territory and is inspired by our Basque culinary heritage and seasonality.*

× **Where do you come from?**

ENEKO ATXA: *I come from a home where we were taught to enjoy the table, the food, the conversation, to learn and enjoy what took place in the kitchen – hence my love for cuisine.*

Eneko Atxa

I HAVE ALWAYS ASSOCIATED THE BEST MOMENTS OF MY CHILDHOOD AND YOUTH WITH THE KITCHEN, WHICH WAS THE NERVE CENTRE OF MY HOUSE.

× **How and when did you become passionate about food?**

ENEKO ATXA: *I have always associated the best moments of my childhood and youth with the kitchen, which was the nerve centre of my house. My mother and grandmother cooked and all the rest of us enjoyed the food. This association always reminds me that pleasure and cuisine go hand in hand.*

× **Which cuisines have influenced your cooking?**

ENEKO ATXA: *I trained at the culinary school in Leioa and later in various restaurants, from traditional Basque restaurants to three-starred Michelin restaurants, such as Martin Berasategui's. All of them had a very positive influence on me. I continue to improve thanks to people who surround me and work with me, and other colleagues.*

× **What are the characteristics of the dishes you like to cook?**

ENEKO ATXA: *They are connected with the environment, seasonality, my taste memory, and my way of understanding or seeing the world through cooking. Beauty is also important to me. I try to create a cuisine rooted in our own territory, and try to make it naturalistic through very pure flavours.*

× **Does a dish have a calling, according to you? And if so, what is it?**

ENEKO ATXA: *The vocation of a dish is clear to me: it has to reflect a landscape, a territory, a culture. In short, a dish, from my perspective, has to tell you where you are. And exalt the characteristics of the environment where it is created.*

× **What are your three favourite ingredients?**

ENEKO ATXA: *It's impossible to choose only three ingredients; each season offers wonderful products. If I had to highlight some, I would opt for those that are in serious danger of extinction.*

× **What is your best quality as a chef?**

ENEKO ATXA: *Work, illusion, persistence and perfectionism.*

× **And what is your shortcoming as a chef?**

ENEKO ATXA: *I have many. I am very insistent in the search for improvement and that sometimes leads me to dwell on an idea so insistently that it sometimes causes tremendous dissatisfaction.*

× **What is your main concern: originality or respect for tradition?**

ENEKO ATXA: *Everyone interprets their own cuisine, which is marked from a territory, from a way of understanding and transmitting the values that each one has. My advice would be: forget trends, do the best you can, no matter whether it's traditional or local cuisine. The only thing that matters, is to be honest, and to offer a good cuisine with personality. I also believe that we should all have a differentiating value: the more different cuisines there are, the more pluralistic and better gastronomy will be.*

ENEKO ATXA - AZURMENDI

Teardrop peas and Iberian gel.

SERVES 225

FOR THE HAM BROTH

10kg ham bones
600g ham trimmings
15L water

Clean the ham bones, removing all the yellow fat. Place the bones together with the ham trimmings and put them in a pot. Cover with water. Reduce over a very low heat for two days, repeatedly removing the foam and any fat that is released. Strain and reduce on a griddle until the desired flavour is achieved.

FOR THE HAM GEL

500g ham broth
6g xanthan gum

Using a blender, thicken the ham broth with the xanthan gum, then remove the air at least three times in a vacuum machine. The amount of xanthan gum required will vary according to the consistency of the ham broth, so more gum may have to be added create the ham gel.

FOR THE MUSHROOM TARTLET

3kg snow pea powder
3kg water
300g isomalt
150g glucose
45g salt
300g maltodextrin
75g cornflour
75g mushroom powder
butter spray

Dry the snow peas in a dehydrator at 60 °C (140 °F) for 24 hours. Grind to make a very fine powder, then add to a saucepan along with the rest of the ingredients except the maltodextrin. Cook for 20 minutes and process until you have a smooth dough. Stretch the dough thinly on a silicone baking mat and put it in the oven at 110 °C (230 °F) for 2 hours without ventilation. Remove and leave to rest for 12 hours. Using a cookie cutter, cut into circles.

Prepare a reducer with warm oil, and with the help of tweezers introduce the circles so that the dough softens (5 seconds approx.).

Remove excess oil by passing the dough along the edges of the reducer, then place the soft circles between two flanera moulds already greased with butter spray. Make sure that the baking paper is well centred and cover with another mould. Bake at 180 °C (356 °F) for 3 minutes with ventilation at mark 3. Unmould, making sure that the base of the tartlet is flat; if not, flatten the base with the help of tongs. To finish drying, place in an oven on parchment paper at 90 °C without ventilation. Keep the tartlets warm.

FOR THE CHIVE OIL
(FOR 70 SERVINGS)

170g chives
700g sunflower oil

Using a Thermomix, blend the oil with the chives for 10 minutes at 40 °C on speed 8. Put a fine strainer over a container and strain the oil overnight. The next day, pass the oil through a Superbag and reserve.

FOR THE CHIVE EMULSION

3 eggs
1.2kg chive oil
caesium salt

Put the eggs and the salt in the glass of the Thermomix.
Blend at speed 3, gradually adding the chive oil until you obtain an emulsion. Add a pinch of salt.

OTHER INGREDIENTS

18g teardrop peas
salad burnet flowers
afilia
dried thyme

TO PLATE

Presentation requires a wooden bowl with a wooden lid.
Stick two tartlets together using a dab of chive emulsion. On top of the second tartlet, add more chive emulsion.
Add the hot ham broth to the wooden bowl then add 3 drops of sherry. Next to the bowl, set a little dried thyme (when the dish is ready to be served, this will be set light to and the dish covered quickly with the lid so that the smoke does not go away).
At the time of the pass, blanch the peas in boiling water. Take out and put in a reducer together with the ham gel and the chive oil (pay careful attention to the cooking of the peas – they should explode in your mouth). Season with salt if necessary.
Cover the tartlet with peas. Place the afilia and the salad burnet flowers on the peas. Place the tartlet on the napkin covering the lid.

José Avillez.

BELCANTO, LISBON (PT)

Born in Lisbon in 1979, Avillez is a well-known face on Portuguese TV for his cooking show and cookbooks. His food empire harbours a cluster of restaurants in Lisbon and Porto, including 2 stars Belcanto, which he opened in 2012.

—— 'This dish talks about my Portuguese roots and childhood,' explains Avillez, who grew up between the ocean and a pine forest in Cascais, a charming seaside town near Lisbon. 'Because the sea is so important to me, I wanted to capture the feeling of taking a dip in its water. "Dip in the Sea" is one of my first signature dishes; it captures the purest sea flavour and pays tribute to the amazing Portuguese fish. I've kept it throughout the years because for me this dish reflects a kind of perfection: it is subtle, elegant and unique.'

Avillez, who started cooking at home at age seven ('I used to bake with my sister, selling the cakes to family, friends and neighbours'), learned his trade at many fine-dining restaurants around the world, including Ferran Adrià's elBulli. 'I've been influenced by all the great chefs I worked with and learned from, especially Ferran Adrià, who played a life-changing role in my career,' explains Avillez. 'He taught me how to think and break down the mental barriers I faced.' Today he follows a simple set of guiding principles – flavour is the most important thing; technique serves the product; the ingredients should be carefully chosen to create incredibly poetic dishes.

Avillez's other great influence is Portuguese cuisine. 'The differentiating aspect of Portuguese cuisine has to do with the cultural exchanges that happened during our Age of Discoveries,' he explains. 'For this reason, our cuisine has some fusion and influences from Africa and Asia. The Portuguese were responsible for the first globalisation phenomenon, all these influences being possible thanks to our spirit of openness to the world. My cuisine intends to reflect that openness.'

Avillez stood out in the fine-dining scene in 2018, when he took on the role of executive chef at Lisbon's landmark restaurant Tavares, where he won his first Michelin star only a year later. The Belcanto adventure started in 2012 and today the leading Portuguese chef has several restaurants in Lisbon, Cascais and Porto, as well as one in Dubai, each one expressing his vision through a different concept.

JOSÉ AVILLEZ - BELCANTO

A Dip in the Sea.

SERVES 4

FOR THE SEA BASS

4 sea bass fillets, deboned, with skin, 180g each

Pack each sea bass fillet in a sous-vide plastic bag and seal it. Set aside in the refrigerator.

FOR THE BIVALVES

650g mussels
325g cockles
650g razor clams
sea salt
150ml mineral water

MUSSELS

Wash the mussels under running water., then, with a table knife, scrape the mussels to remove any dirt from the shell. Each time you wash the mussels under running water, follow this up by submerging them in a 2-per-cent brine (1 litre of water per 20g of salt). Lay the mussels in a baking tray and add the mineral water, and cook for 10–12 minutes in a steam oven preheated to 100 ºC (210 ºF). Remove the tray from the oven, transfer the mussels to another tray and set the water aside.
Keep the mussels on the tray for later use.

COCKLES

Wash all the cockles under running water. Put them it in a medium-sized saucepan with boiling water, and cook them for 13 seconds. Using a slotted spoon, immediately transfer the cockles to a tray, placing in the refrigerator to cool. Once cooled, remove the cockles from their shells and place them in a tray in a cold bain-marie while you prepare them. Cut the cockles in half and discard their stomachs. Scrape the sand out of their heads. Set aside the clean cockles in a cup in the refrigerator.

RAZOR CLAMS

Place all the razor clams in medium-sized vacuum bags (20–25 clams per bag), add a little brine to each bag and then seal them, ensuring you have removed all the air. In a large pan with boiling water and room for all the bags, cook the razor clams for 2 minutes. Take the bags out of the water and immediately place them in a container with iced water, so that they quickly cool (approx. 5–10 minutes). Discard the cooking water. Take the bags out of the iced water and open them. Strain the razor clams and place them in a cold bain-marie while you prepare them. Save some of the cooking juices. One by one, open the razor clams, pull the heads out without removing the stomach from the case, and push the body against the razor blade to cut the body, taking care not to cut the stomach. Discard the shell and stomach.
Set the razor clams aside in the cold, inside a lidded plastic container of suitable size, covered with some of the razor clam juices.

JOSÉ AVILLEZ - BELCANTO

FOR THE 'SEA WATER'

100ml mussels' cooking water

Filter the mussels' cooking water through a fine-mesh sieve. Let cool and set aside.

FOR THE SEAWEED AND MARINE PLANTS

160g sea lettuce
160g red tosaka
160g green tosaka
70g green sea fingers (Codium fragile)
75g sea grapes (Caulerpa lentillifera)

SEA LETTUCE

In a medium saucepan over a high heat, heat some water with salt and bring it to boil. Once the water is boiling, blanch the sea lettuce for 5 seconds. Take it out of the water using tweezers or a skimmer and immerse immediately in a container with iced, salted water.
Once cooled, take the sea lettuce out of the water and, leaf by leaf, make sure that it is washed (with no sand, etc.) and that there are no large holes.
Drain the leaves and store it in a plastic box lined with moistened paper towels. Repeat the process for all leaves. Cover the leaves with slightly damp paper towels, place the lid on the plastic container and store in the cold until needed.

RED TOSAKA

Take the red tosaka seaweed out of its package and wash under running water to remove any excess salt. Place the red tosaka seaweed in a container with water for 5 minutes, for desalting.
After this time, check whether it needs further desalting. Strain the red tosaka in a fine-mesh sieve, dry it on paper towels and set aside it in the cold in a plastic box, lined and covered with moistened paper towels.

GREEN TOSAKA

Take the green tosaka seaweed out of its package and wash under running water to remove any excess salt. Place the green tosaka seaweed in a container with water for 5 minutes, for desalting. After this time, check whether it needs further desalting. Strain the green tosaka in a fine-mesh sieve, and then blanch it in hot water for 2–5 seconds. Transfer the green tosaka to a container with iced, salted water. When cooled, take it out, dry it on paper towels and set it aside in the cold, in a plastic box lined and covered with moistened paper towels.

GREEN SEA FINGERS (CODIUM FRAGILE)

Open the package and transfer the sea fingers to a tray lined with sturdy paper towels. Let them breathe in the refrigerator for about 4–5 hours.
At the time of preparation, cut and trim the sea fingers to form various 'Y' shapes. In a fine-mesh sieve, pass under cold running water, to remove the gum.
Dry on sturdy paper towels and set aside in the cold, in a plastic box lined and covered with moistened paper towels.

SEA GRAPES (CAULERPA LENTILLIFERA)

In a stainless-steel container with cold water, soak the sea grapes for 3 minutes. Then, cut them into 1.5cm portions. Make a brine (25g of salt to 1 litre of water) in a small plastic container and place the cut sea grapes inside it. Set aside in the cold.

TO FINISH AND PLATE

lemon juice to taste

Place the sea bass (sealed in a sous-vide bag) in a bain-marie heated to 54 °C (129 °F), for 25–27 minutes.
Heat the bivalves, the sea lettuce and the tosaka in a seawater steam.
Heat the 100ml of sea water (the mussel broth) in a saucepan to 80 °C (769 °F). Before plating, taste and season with 3 drops of lemon juice.
In a deep dish, place the sea bass fillet at the centre. On top, put the sea lettuce and all the bivalves, without overlapping them.
Also place the tosakas, the sea grape and the sea fingers. Pour some sea water onto the bottom of the dish and on top of the fish.

Ivan & Sergey Berezutsky.

(FORMERLY) TWINS GARDEN, MOSCOW (RU)

Following the success of their debut restaurant, brothers Ivan and Sergey Berezutsky were chefs at Twin Gardens from 2017 until 2023. Their award-winning team sourced most of its products from its own farm and cooked up wonders in its hi-tech lab.

—— Part of the Rediscover Russia degustation menu, the Berezutskys' signature dish is called 'Armavir', after the twin brothers' hometown in the south of Russia. 'It's a 3D-flower made of potato skin paste with a butterfly made of smoked beef and pork fat trimmings, served on marinated coral milky cap mushrooms and mustard seed sauce,' the twins explain. 'This dish is all about us; its taste comes from our childhood. Our mother used to bake potatoes and then serve them with slices of frozen lard. It was one of our favourite dishes.'

The brothers grew up helping their mum in the kitchen. 'One of our favourite childhood memories is baking cookies with mum (oh, that smell in the kitchen!) or making a traditional sauce called adjika,' recall the chefs, who also helped their mum in the garden: 'We remember the taste and aroma of fresh tomatoes and herbs; far superior to vegetables from the supermarket. Our dream was to share these memories with our guests in our restaurant and this is the reason we had our own farm providing Twins Garden with the freshest vegetables in season.

'This dish looks simple, yet behind it is our "nature meets science" philosophy,' explain the brothers. 'We use both local Russian seasonal products and modern culinary science. The potato flower is made of potato peels using a 3D-printer, which helps give the flower a unique porous structure to absorb melting fat. The butterfly is made of beef and pork fat trimmings, typical restaurant food waste. We keep the trimmings, smoke them slightly, then melt and freeze them in the form of a butterfly.' The dish is usually served with morel wine, a unique product found only at Twins Garden. 'We also make other mushroom, vegetable, herb and seaweed wines.'

This philosophy was developed after extensive training at some of the world's top restaurants. Ivan trained at elBulli in Spain, while Sergey trained at the legendary Alinea in Chicago. Chef Ferran Adrià taught them the most: 'The main thing we learned from him is the "no borders" concept. Nothing is impossible. Our favourite question is "Why not?"'

IVAN & SERGEY BEREZUTSKY - (FORMERLY) TWINS GARDEN

Armavir. *(3D-printed potato flower with smoked lard butterfly)*

SERVES 1

FOR THE POTATO FLOWERS

100g potato skin purée
10g Parmesan cheese, finely grated
10g potato starch
30g egg
salt and black pepper

Wash the potato peel, and bake in the oven until crunchy and golden brown. Add water to the baked skins and cook until soft, blend the skins and pass through a sieve, add some water if needed (you can also add some regular mashed potatoes for a smoother texture). To make the potato skin purée, mix the baked skins with the egg, potato starch and Parmesan, season with salt and pepper, then pass the mixture through a sieve. Put into a 3D-printer and print a flower with a porous structure. Steam the flower at 100 °C (210 °F) for 15 minutes. Allow to cool then deep-fry at 150 °C (120 °F) until golden brown. Put onto paper towels to absorb excess oil, and season with salt flakes.

FOR THE MUSTARD SAUCE

30g grain mustard
15g shallots
30g honey
8g white wine
10g olive oil
salt and black pepper

Cut shallots into small cubes, mix together all the ingredients, and season with salt and pepper.

FOR THE SMOKED-LARD BUTTERFLIES

70% beef fat trimmings
30% pork fat trimmings
10g fat in total for 1 butterfly

Cut the fat trimmings into small pieces and smoke. Put the smoked fat in a vacuum plastic bag, vacuumie and cook at 100 °C (210 °F) until totally melted. Sieve the hot melted fat and cool down until creamy. Put the creamy fat into silicone butterfly moulds and freeze until solid. Take the butterflies out of the moulds. Take a serving knife, drop some fat on it and stick a frozen butterfly on it. Keep in a freezer until ready to serve.

FOR THE CORAL MILK CAP MUSHROOMS

10g marinated coral milk cap mushrooms
1g chives
3g unrefined sunflower oil

Cut the marinated coral milky cap mushrooms and chives into small pieces, then mix with the sunflower oil.

TO PLATE

Put some mustard sauce in the middle of a plate, add some of the coral milk cap mushrooms mix, and cover with a potato flower with a little more mustard sauce in the middle. After a short presentation of the dish, put the butterfly on top of the flower from the serving knife. The butterfly melts in 30 seconds and soaks the flower.
Serve with morel wine, a wine made with morels. At Twins Garden vegetable, mushroom, herb and flower wines are made, using traditional vinification technology. Wine fermentation provides a unique morel aroma and flavour.

Massimo Bottura.

OSTERIA FRANCESCANA, MODENA (IT)

Massimo Bottura was born in 1962 in Modena, where he took over the traditional Osteria Francescana in 1995. His three Michelin star restaurant was twice voted the best restaurant in the world, and with his wife Lara, the chef is the co-founder of the non-profit project Food for Soul, which promotes social awareness about food waste and hunger.

—— Massimo Bottura found it 'almost impossible' to decide on his signature dish, but eventually settled for his Five Ages of Parmigiano Reggiano in different textures and temperatures, an elaborate dish which made history (and a star appearance on *Chef's Table*).

'This dish began to take shape over 30 years ago, before I opened Osteria Francescana,' explains Bottura. 'It then became its essence and soul, and has been part of the menu since the restaurant's opening in 1995. Today, it's part of the Francescana at Maria Luigia dining experience at our guesthouse Casa Maria Luigia in the Emilian countryside.'

Back in 1986, Bottura opened Trattoria del Campazzo. 'I was a young chef back then, but I had a clear idea of how I wanted to represent Emilia-Romagna in my cuisine, respecting the territory but filtering it through a contemporary mind,' he says. 'I was convinced that Parmigiano Reggiano was the one ingredient able to paint a portrait of the region; I just had to find a way to bring it into a dish. So, I began to experiment and transform this incredible cheese in a way that nobody had ever done before.' The result was 'Three textures and temperatures of Parmigiano Reggiano', but it was just the beginning. 'It evolved with me as I developed as a chef, and digging deep into my roots I discovered that Parmigiano Reggiano was not just any old cheese, but a living and breathing portrait of Emilia-Romagna, with its fog, humidity and deep respect for the passing of time.'

Later iterations involved four, then finally five ages of parmesan. 'It was no longer made with only one ingredient, but two: Parmigiano Reggiano and time,' says Bottura. The iconic dish is a celebration of the region, its climate and of the cheesemakers from the Apennines to the Po River, embodied in a stunning 'white-on-white monochrome' bathed in 'fog' and gathering five different ages of the cheese: a 24-month, 30-month, 36-month, 40-month, and a 50-month aged Parmigiano Reggiano.

MASSIMO BOTTURA - OSTERIA FRANCESCANA

Five ages of Parmigiano Reggiano in different textures and at different temperatures.

SERVES 4

FOR THE PARMESAN
DEMI-SOUFFLÉ

200g organic ricotta
60g egg white
100g 24-month Parmigiano Reggiano, grated
40g double (heavy) cream
1g sea salt
0.5g white pepper, ground

Grease some 8 x 4-cm aluminium timbales. Smoke the ricotta lightly over cherry-wood chips in a sealed oven for 3 minutes.
Whisk the egg white to stiff peaks.
Whip the ricotta. Mix the Parmesan with the cream, combine with the ricotta, and season with the salt and pepper. Fold in the whisked egg white and steam in the timbales for 45 minutes. Remove from the timbales and shape the soufflés into quenelles.

FOR THE PARMESAN SAUCE

20g capon stock, not strained
100g 30-month Parmigiano Reggiano, grated

Bring the stock to 60 °C (140 °F) at medium speed in a thermal mixer. Add the Parmesan and bring the mixture to 85 °C (185 °F). Increase the speed and process to create a smooth, velvety sauce. Pass through a fine chinois.

FOR THE PARMESAN FOAM

125g capon stock
25g 36-month Parmigiano Reggiano, grated
100g double (heavy) cream

Put the capon stock in a thermal mixer and bring to a boil at setting 3. Add the Parmesan a spoonful at a time. Increase the speed for 1 more minute, then add the cream. Cool the mixture to 4–8 °C (39–46 °F). Place in a syphon, shake it, charge it with a double cartridge and shake again. Allow to rest in the refrigerator for at least 1 hour at 4–8 °C (39–46 °F) before serving.

FOR THE PARMESAN WAFER

100g 40-month Parmigiano Reggiano, grated
100g mineral water

Put the Parmesan and water in a pan and slowly bring to a boil until the cheese becomes stringy. Remove from the heat and allow to rest at room temperature for 2 hours. Drain off the liquid and put the cheese in the refrigerator overnight. Preheat the oven to 170 °C (325 °F). Roll out the cold cheese dough to a thickness of 1mm and lay it out flat on a silicone baking mat. Bake for 12 minutes until it is a thin wafer. Cool at room temperature, then crack it into four parts. Break into imperfect 5cm equilateral triangles.

FOR THE PARMESAN AIR

200g 50-month Parmigiano Reggiano crusts
200g 50-month Parmigiano Reggiano, grated
2g lecithin
500g water

Place the Parmesan crusts in a pan with 500g water and simmer for 3 hours over a low heat. Strain and cool the liquid. Blend the chilled liquid and the grated Parmigiano for 30 minutes, then let it rest in the fridge overnight. Strain it through a tamis sieve and transfer the strained liquid to a large bowl. Just before serving, add the lecithin and whisk with a hand blender until it rises into a cloud of air.

TO PLATE

Place two quenelles of demi-soufflé at the base of each plate and add two spoonfuls of sauce around the soufflé. Place the foam on top, add a wafer at a diagonal slant, and finally a cloud of air covering one quarter of the plate.

Manu Buffara.

MANU, CURITIBA (BR)

Born in Curitiba in 1983, Manu Buffara is the chef and owner of Manu, a restaurant celebrating the unique culture and produce of the region of Paraná. A champion of sustainability, and named Latin America's Best Female Chef 2022, Buffara is involved in local community initiatives such as Alimenta Curitiba and Urban Gardens. She is due to open her second restaurant, Ella, in New York's Meatpacking District by the end of 2023.

× What does your signature dish tell us about you?

MANU BUFFARA: *This dish says a lot about my cuisine, due to the simplicity of the ingredients and the intensity of its flavours. It also represents my techniques very well: the cauliflower is steamed, served with a passion fruit sauce, peanut butter and bottarga. What I really love about this recipe is the combination of the sour passion fruit, the umami that comes from the way we cook the cauliflower and the unusual addition of peanuts, rarely used by chefs, but one of the most incredible indigenous Brazilian ingredients.*

× What is the story behind its creation?

MANU BUFFARA: *This dish is made of products from my land. I usually find the passion fruit, peanuts and cauliflower in the street markets of my city, while the bottarga is from the region of Morretes in Paraná. These ingredients carry a little of my history.*

× Where do you come from?

MANU BUFFARA: *I come from the countryside of Paraná, and I believe that food is the engine that connects me to the land, my people, my family and the planet. I fight for the quality of the food, its diversity of ingredients, and for the work of our local farmers. My food is a way of defending my philosophy and a way of telling a story.*

> FOR ME COOKING IS AN EXPRESSION OF LOVE, KNOWLEDGE, TECHNIQUE, AUTHENTICITY AND RESPECT.

× **How would you describe your cooking and the philosophy behind it?**

MANU BUFFARA: *For me cooking is an expression of love, knowledge, technique, authenticity and respect. Respect for the product, for the farmer, for the chef, for my apron and my family. My relationship with the vegetables is deep because they are my inspiration. I know each ingredient I use in my preparations, as well as the story behind each one.*

× **How and when did you become passionate about food?**

MANU BUFFARA: *I've always had a very strong connection to food, and especially where it comes from, through my family. That became a profession when I was 18.*

× **Which cuisines influence your cooking?**

MANU BUFFARA: *The cuisines that most influenced me were those of my Lebanese and Italian grandmothers, and the Caiçara cuisine of my family from Paranaguá on the coast of Paraná.*

× **What are the characteristics of the dishes you like to cook?**

MANU BUFFARA: *Dishes with vegetables and ingredients from the sea. My relationship with vegetables is deep; they are my source of inspiration.*

× **What are your three favourite ingredients?**

MANU BUFFARA: *At the moment they are cashew nuts, tucupi and peanuts from Mr Divonei, a producer here in the region.*

× **What is your main source of inspiration?**

MANU BUFFARA: *Mainly from the people around me, from my daughters, from travel, from my products and producers.*

× **What is your main concern: originality or respect for tradition?**

MANU BUFFARA: *I believe in both. We need originality in everything we do, and respect for people, the earth and the planet is essential.*

× **What chefs do you admire?**

MANU BUFFARA: *I admire many chefs, among whom Alex Atala, René Redzepi, Mauro Colagreco, Ana Roš, Jorge Vallejo, Virgilio Martínez and Pía León, Narisawa.*

MANU BUFFARA - MANU

Cauliflower, passionfruit and peanuts.

SERVES 4

FOR THE CAULIFLOWER

1 small cauliflower
50g butter
150ml water

Choose a pan large enough to hold the cauliflower. Heat the butter until it is sizzling. and sear the cauliflower on every side. Pour in the water. Cover and allow to cook through completely (10–15 minutes). If the liquid has evaporated in the middle of cooking, add another 150ml water. The cauliflower must be very soft, but not falling apart. Remove the cauliflower from the pan and let it cool, then cut into portions of 1 floret per person. Reserve the liquid.

FOR THE PASSIONFRUIT FRIED MILK

300g unsalted butter
150g cauliflower, cut into chunks
200g whole milk
110g passionfruit (only juice and seeds)
100g brown butter
120g whole milk
50g double cream

Heat the butter until it is sizzling and add the cauliflower chunks. Allow to cook at a low temperature for 1 hour, then drain. In a tall pan, bring the cauliflower butter (185g) to the boil again and fry the milk (it will rise to the surface). Add the passionfruit, blend for 5 minutes, and set aside to rest. Next bring the brown butter to boil in another tall pan. Fry the milk and the heavy cream, and allow to boil for 3 minutes. Blend until smooth. Then add the passionfruit mixture and blend it again at maximum power for 2 minutes until homogenised.

FOR THE PEANUT FOAM

300g peanuts
350g whole milk
200g double cream
50g rice vinegar
a pinch of salt

Preheat the oven at 180 °C (355 °F) and toast the peanuts lightly (around 10 minutes). Blend the peanuts and milk to a homogeneous paste. Pass through a tamis sieve. Bring the mixture to a bare simmer in a pan and add the double cream. Remove from the heat and add the vinegar and salt. Blend with a mixer while still warm. Pass through a tamis sieve again and put in a syphon bottle with 2 charges. Set it aside in the refrigerator for at least 4 hours. Take out of the syphon and put into a squeeze bottle.

TO PLATE

In a medium-size pan, heat the cauliflower liquid reserved from the cooking of the cauliflower, add the cauliflower, and cook on a high heat for 5 minutes. In a bowl, add the passionfruit milk, then add the cauliflower in the middle, and cover with the cauliflower liquid. Put the peanut foam next to the cauliflower and finish with a pinch of salt. Serve with a tiny slice of bottarga and a little fried sage.

Riccardo Camanini.

LIDO 84, BRESCIA (IT)

Born in 1973 in Northern Italy, Riccardo Camanini trained with Raymond Blanc and Hélène Darroze before opening his own restaurant at age 40 with the help of his brother Giancarlo. Lido 84, on Lake Garda, is now a must-visit gourmet destination.

—— As a child growing up in a small village near Bergamo, Lombardy, Riccardo Camanini was happier on the football pitch than in the kitchen. But he fell in love with the world of fine dining at age 19 after a stint with legendary Italian chef Gualtiero Marchesi. Since then, the chef has immersed himself in the art and history of gastronomy, as his signature dish exemplifies.

'The idea was born while reading *De re Coquinaria* (Of Culinary Matters), a book by Marcus Gavius Apicius and probably the first recipe book of which we have historical knowledge. Apicius was a wealthy Roman merchant, who lived during the time of Emperor Tiberius,' says Camanini. 'He wrote that the food was stored inside pig bladders to facilitate transportation from one colony to another. From this, various thoughts began to emerge in my mind, several references to preparations and gestures, and possible usage of the bladder. So I thought: why not try it with pasta?'

Camanini's cacio e pepe en vessie is 'a cultural bridge between Italy and Scottish and German gastronomic preparations, where internal organs are used for cooking food.' Created after much experimentation, it's a mash-up of Rome's simple but iconic cacio e pepe pasta (its cheese and black pepper sauce has just enough liquid to steam the pasta) and the traditional cooking method 'en vessie', (in a bladder), made famous by the Scots and their haggis. The result is a show-stopping dish for four that arrives at the table as a large inflated ball, which is then punctured by a server to reveal a portion of steaming rigatoni, perfectly cooked and coated in the pepper and cheese sauce.

The dining experience is both theatrical and artisanal – and possibly one of the most Instagrammed in Italy. Yet this is not about a polished, seamless experience: 'It's like when you buy shoes from an artisan,' Camanini has said, 'you find these imperfections because they're handmade. Cuisines need to be like this.' With one foot in the past and one foot in the future, Camanini's signature dish is certainly one for the history books.

RICCARDO CAMANINI - LIDO 84

Cacio e pepe pasta en vessie.

SERVES 4

INGREDIENTS

1 dehydrated pig's bladder
300g rigatoni (Riccardo recommends using the Felicetti brand as it is resilient enough to withstand the 30 minutes' cooking time)
135g pecorino nero (aged black-rind variety), grated
90g extra-virgin olive oil
3g black pepper, freshly cracked
12g salt (Riccardo uses Guérande)

Soak the dehydrated pig's bladder in cold water for about 10 days, changing the water daily. When the bladder is adequately hydrated, insert the other ingredients into it using a funnel, then firmly secure the bladder opening with kitchen twine.

Cook the stuffed bladder in a large pan of boiling water, being sure to keep it submerged in the water and shaking it occasionally to mix the pasta inside. Cook for 30 minutes.

TO PLATE

Serve in front of guests by cutting open the bladder with a sharp knife and spooning the rigatoni onto plates.

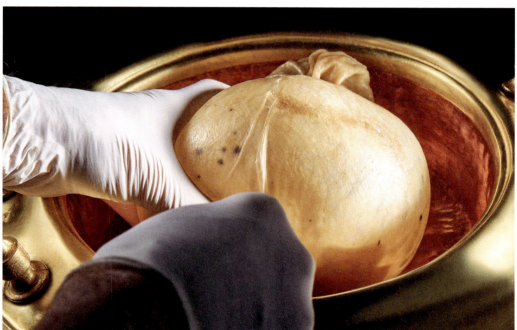
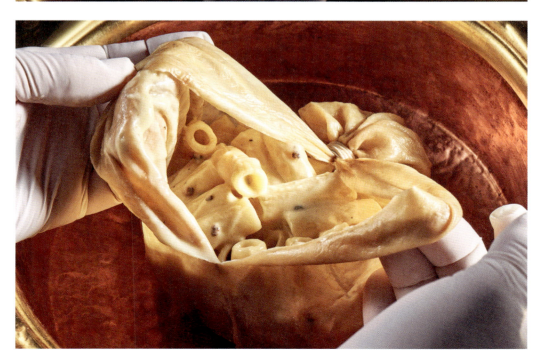

Mateu Casañas, Oriol Castro & Eduard Xatruch.

DISFRUTAR, BARCELONA (ES)

Spanish chefs Eduard Xatruch, Oriol Castro and Mateu Casañas met while working at elBulli with Ferran Adrià. The trio opened Compartir in Cadaqués in 2012, followed by Disfrutar in Barcelona in 2014, exploring contemporary techniques and daring combinations, with the latter now boasting two Michelin stars.

—— Hailing from Girona, Barcelona and Tarragona respectively, Mateu Casañas, Oriol Castro and Eduard Xatruch opened their restaurant in Barcelona after spending over 15 years experimenting with cutting-edge gastronomy in the kitchens of elBulli. Their dish of panchino filled with caviar and sour cream perfectly represents their focus on innovation.

'There is no doubt that this dish has become a signature Disfrutar creation, both in terms of the pleasure it brings when it's eaten and for the contribution it has made in a technical sense,' say the chefs. 'The method of deep-frying batter foams allows us to make buns with a texture similar to that of the finest brioche, which we fill immediately before frying with all sorts of fresh, frozen, sweet and savoury products.

'The technique emerged in the restaurant's creative workshop, thanks to the research work we do there every day,' the chefs continue. 'Our philosophy is to never stop. To keep on working every day in search of new techniques and new concepts. We are driven by this restlessness.'

Served with truffle-infused vodka, the panchino — also known as the caviar bun, inspired by the Chinese bao — is meant to be an explosion of flavour and texture in your mouth, while the smooth and delicate brioche contrasts beautifully with the grains of the caviar.

Disfrutar, which translates as 'enjoy', offers a tasting menu of playful and innovative cuisine and its dishes stand out for their distinctly Mediterranean identity. 'What appeals to us about a dish is to have no reference: it should throw you off and break the register, seeking to express something new', say the chefs. Unsurprisingly, their menu was once described as a 'roller-coaster ride of a dining experience.' As well as the caviar-filled fluffy panchino, there are dishes of spherical pesto with pistachio and eels, gazpacho sandwiches and chocolate peppers with oil and salt.

'We like to cook with products — dried fruit, parmesan, prawns, local produce — and combine them to evolve,' say the trio, who have been influenced by many cuisines, in particular Japanese gastronomy, for 'its sensitivity and passion for the product. It's like poetry and we love it.'

MATEU CASAÑAS, ORIOL CASTRO & EDUARD XATRUCH - DISFRUTAR

Panchino filled with caviar and sour cream.

SERVES 10

FOR THE SOURED CREAM

200g cream (35% fat)
20g natural yoghurt

Mix the cream with the yoghurt, then transfer the mixture to the ceramic pot of the OCOO double boiler. Run the fermentation programme for 21 hours.
Place a sieve lined with kitchen paper over a container, pour in the soured cream and leave to drain off the excess whey in the refrigerator for 3 hours. Transfer to an airtight container and set aside in the refrigerator.

FOR THE PANCHINO BATTER FOAM

240g pasteurised egg
150g water
290g flour
60g sugar
16g rosemary honey

Combine all the ingredients in a container and process with a handheld blender until lump-free. Strain and transfer to a 1L syphon. Close the syphon and insert 3 N_2O gas cartridges. Refrigerate for 3 hours.

ADDITIONAL INGREDIENTS

130g beluga caviar
2kg sunflower oil

FINISHING AND PREPARATION

Heat the oil in a pan to 200 °C (392 °F).
Put 13g of caviar and 4g of sour cream into each of 10 tablespoons.
Dip a 4.5-cm-diameter metal ladle into the oil for 10 seconds to heat well. Pour out the oil and pipe the panchino batter foam into the centre of the ladle, covering the base.
Quickly put the caviar and sour cream contained in a spoon into the centre of the foam.
Cover the filling with batter foam and then dip the ladle into the hot oil. The foam ball will automatically detach itself from the ladle and keep its round shape. Fry for 15 seconds, then use a skimmer to turn it over and fry for 15 more seconds.
Carefully drain the filled Panchino and dry it very well with kitchen paper. Serve.

SIGNATURE DISHES — 69

Vicky Cheng.

VEA, HONG KONG (CN)

Born in Hong Kong and raised in Canada, Vicky Cheng combines Asian products and French techniques at Vea, the counter restaurant he founded in his hometown in 2011.

⸺ 'This is the first signature dish I ever did that reflects Vea's culinary philosophy,' says Vicky Cheng about his roasted sea cucumber recipe. 'It symbolises a bridge between my Chinese roots and French culinary training, as it embraces the exquisiteness and preciseness of modern French techniques, while giving the Chinese dried seafood a new presentation and flavour. This dish represents Vea's Chinese x French philosophy, and my own background as a chef who was born in Hong Kong and trained under some of the most respected French chefs.'

Cheng hopes the dish appeals both to locals keen to try a new twist on traditional products, and novices who want to discover more about local delicacies. The dried sea cucumber is dipped in hot oil to create a crispy outer layer — a departure from the traditional Chinese cooking method, in which the sea cucumber is normally braised to a soft, chewy texture. In Cheng's unique version, 'the sea cucumber is stuffed with tiger prawn mousseline, served with a sauce made using the shell and head of the prawn and finished with a fine mist of 20-year-old Shaoxing wine from Hong Kong.'

So why does Cheng want to focus on this dried seafood? 'I want our guests to experience Vea as a story that represents Hong Kong, whether it's in the form of a local song, an ingredient or even plateware. Dried seafood is a widely used luxurious ingredient in Chinese restaurants just like caviar and truffle in the west, he explains. 'But even though the appearance may look Chinese, the taste and flavour is ultimately French. This is why I believe it ticks all the boxes to be used in a fine-dining restaurant with Chinese x French philosophy.'

Cheng, who fell in love with cooking while watching cookery shows on TV, finds inspiration everywhere: 'It can come from finding an ingredient in the market, watching a video or reading a book, or tasting other people's dishes — not only fine-dining dishes but more casual traditional Chinese dishes.' The chef has recently opened a Chinese restaurant, Wing, where he continues to experiment with other contemporary Chinese favourites such as dried fish maw and dried abalone.

VICKY CHENG - VEA

Roasted sea cucumber.

SERVES 4 - 6

FOR THE DRIED
SEA CUCUMBER

Day 1: Soak the dried sea cucumber in water in the refrigerator for 2 days.

Day 3: Strain, place the sea cucumber in a pan of boiling water, then bring back to the boil. Remove from the heat, cover and leave at room temperature for 24 hours.

Day 4: Strain, then clean the outsides of the sea cucumber with the back of knife until free of black tissue. Place the sea cucumber in a pan of boiling water and bring back to the boil. Remove from the heat, cover and leave at room temperature for 24 hours.

Day 5: Strain, cut open the stomach and remove the insides. Place the sea cucumber in a pan of boiling water and bring back to the boil. Remove from the heat, cover and leave at room temperature for 24 hours.

Day 6: Pipe with the shrimp mousse (see below) and steam for 5 minutes, then allow to cool, remove from the plastic and reserve.

FOR THE SHRIMP MOUSSE

100g scallop
200g prawn meat, diced
45g egg white
90g cream
50g prawn meat, chopped
salt and white pepper, to taste

In a Robot-Coupe (or similar), food-process the scallop. Add the egg white, salt and pepper, then pass through a fine sieve.
Place the resulting purée in a bowl over ice. Slowly pour in the cream, fold in the prawn meat, and season with salt and pepper.

OTHER INGREDIENTS

1L vegetable oil
Shaoxing wine

TO PLATE

Ladle hot oil over the top of the sea cucumber until crispy. Place the sea cucumber in the middle of plate or bowl. Pour the prawn sauce around, then mist with Shaoxing wine and serve immediately.

Andre Chiang.

RAW, TAIPEI (TW) AND SICHUAN MOON, MACAU (CN)

Born in Taiwan, André Chiang spent a couple of years in Japan before honing his skills in France, working with chefs such as Michel Troisgros and Joël Robuchon. He is the former head chef of the three Michelin star restaurant Le Jardin des Sens in France, and the two Michelin-star Restaurant André in Singapore. Known for his Octaphilosophy of eight elements, the Taiwanese chef runs restaurants in Taipei and Chengdu.

—— 'This signature dish is also called "Memory 1997" because it represents the very first dish of my own creation, born in 1997,' explains André Chiang. 'It is memorable for me as it represents the beginning of my creative journey.' At the time, Chiang was working at the Pourcel brothers' Jardin des Sens in Montpellier. 'The team was asked to suggest dishes to be eventually featured on the menu,' he recalls. 'When the Frères Pourcel decided to feature my own dish on their three-Michelin star restaurant menu… I was so proud – it was the beginning of my self-confidence as a chef.'

This dish symbolises a real turning point for Chiang. 'Being an Asian cook, very young, I didn't have so much confidence. That dish marks the moment when I started to take more risks, to try new things.' Although it features two classic French ingredients, truffle and foie gras, it uses them in an innovative way: 'a combination that is super classic yet with an unexpected texture'. Foie gras is often associated with rich, heavy dishes but here it appears in a very light composition, based on chawamushi, a classic steamed savoury egg custard.

The Japanese element stems from his experience living in Japan, where his mum owned a Chinese restaurant. 'One of my first memories is being with her in the kitchen, cooking a traditional soup that we drink in the very cold winter,' says Chiang. 'It is a boiled chicken soup prepared with ginger broth, rice wine and sesame oil. It is emblematic of winter in Taiwan: when you boil this soup the whole room smells of ginger and sesame oil.'

Although he's always been fascinated by French cuisine, Chiang developed his own cooking style, the Octaphilosophy, while working at a luxury resort in the Seychelles. Its eight different 'elements' need to be present in every single of his dishes – the key words being salt, texture, memory, purity, terroir, south artisan and uniqueness. The chef also mentions that his favourite ingredients are anything salty – cured meat, anchovies, soy sauce, while his sources of inspirations remain as varied as ever: 'It could be anything happening around me: a weather change, something environmental, a love story, a challenge that we are facing in life. For me, creating a dish is almost like writing a diary.'

ANDRE CHIANG - RAW (TAIPEI) AND SICHUAN MOON (MACAU)

'Memory 1997': foie gras, truffle, chive.

SERVES 4

FOR THE TRUFFLE COULIS

Olive oil, for frying
500g button mushrooms, cut into 5mm (0,25 inches) slices
30g dried morels
30g dried porcini
1L water
100g onions, sliced
100g shallots, sliced
2 cloves of garlic
150g unsalted butter
1 sprig thyme
Fleur de sel, to taste
600ml chicken stock, reduced to 400ml
12g Japanese cornstarch
80g Perigord black truffle, chopped

For the truffle coulis, heat the oil in a frying pan, then add the mushrooms and let them soften, without colouring. Strain off the 'umami' liquid that is released by the mushrooms through a chinois and reserve for the clarifying juice.
Soak the dried morels and porcini in the water overnight. Strain, reserving the soaking liquid, and fry the rehydrated mushrooms in a little oil until golden. Add the onion, shallots and garlic and wait until coloured. Add the butter and thyme and continue frying until brown and caramelised. Season with fleur de sel then add the reduced chicken stock and the reserved mushroom soaking liquid. Simmer for 3 hours, then strain through a chinois and let cool.

FOR THE FOIE GRAS ROYALE

200g foie gras, at room temperature
50ml cream, at room temperature
4g salt
White pepper

To make the foie gras royale, combine all the ingredients in a mixing bowl with ball whisk. Whisk slow to fast to whip up the foie gras while cooking it with a blowtorch under the mixing bowl; carefully monitor the cooking and speed, it should produce a 'sabayon' or soft 'pâte à bombe' texture after 10 minutes, or until it reaches 50 °C (120 °F). Pour into 10 ramequins immediately and warm in the oven for 40 minutes at 78 °C (172 °F) and lower the temperature to 56 °C (133 °F) for 1 hour before serving.

FOR THE CLARIFYING JUICE

60g button mushrooms
40g onion, coarsely chopped
30g carrot, coarsely chopped
20g green celery, coarsely chopped
60g chicken mince
1 egg white, whipped

To make the clarifying juice, combine the vegetables and chicken in a Thermomix and blend to a smooth paste. Tip into a pan and stir in the whipped egg white and the reserved 'umami' liquid and 300ml of the cooled stock. Bring to a boil, then remove from the heat and rest for 20 minutes. Strain through cheese cloth into a bowl. Thicken with the cornstarch to a syrup consistency then stir in the chopped truffle.

TO GARNISH

Chopped chives
Truffle oil
Extra-virgin olive oil

To serve, remove the warm foie gras custards from the oven and torch the surface of each until slightly browned. Top each with 2,5 table spoons of truffle coulis. Garnish with chopped chives and drops of truffle oil and olive oil.

Paul Chung.

SAISON HOSPITALITY, SAN FRANCISCO (US)

San Francisco native Paul Chung began his career in Michelin-starred restaurants in New York, Chicago, Paris and Seoul. The chef is now the Culinary Director of Saison Hospitality, overseeing the Michelinstarred Saison Hospitality and Angler San Francisco, and Angler Los Angeles.

—— 'This dish is a representation of my cultural upbringing and my love for the California coast,' says Chung of his California urchin gimmari. 'Like myself it has a dual identity; Mendocino's sea urchin is incredibly rich and briny, with a subtle sweetness, yet it truly shines when joined with the rice and the three varieties of Korean seaweed that carry it. It's both native and foreign, traditional and progressive, Korean and American; I believe this dish shines through its complexities.'

The origin of the creation lies in gimmari, a traditional Korean dish that is often found at street food stalls in bustling night markets. 'It's rarely the star of the meal, yet is nonetheless always sought after and served with other items,' explains the chef. 'It's often presented as a variety of seasoned glass noodles wrapped in gim (dried seaweed) and then fried, but other common variations include sautéed vegetables and rice.'

The inspiration behind this dish came to Chung while visiting the Mendocino coast to harvest some seaweed. 'The conditions were perfect and the tide was out by early afternoon,' he recalls. 'I collected an abundance of seaweed and sat next to a tide pool to enjoy my packed lunch of leftover gimmari. But there was a clear richness missing as my meal consisted mostly of rice and preserved vegetables. Luckily, Mendocino is littered with Purple Hotchi urchins – I opened a few and had a gimmari and urchin together for the first time. The roe was very bitter with distinct metallic notes, but when combined with the gimmari there was potential.'

Since then, Chung has replaced the traditional dried laver with *gamtae,* a dried seaweed hand-harvested in the mudflats of Korea, and substituted the glass noodles with California Koshihikari rice cooked with *miyeok* broth and *maesaengi*. The combination of all three seaweeds creates a deep umami savouriness that is well matched to the richness of the fresh urchin. 'In line with our ethos of live-fire cooking at Saison Hospitality, the broken pieces of urchin are gathered together and gently dipped in a solution of smoked tamari. We then gently pack them together with cheesecloth and allow them to slowly dry over our hearth for a week. This process helps compress the broken pieces together while imbuing the urchin with a unique smoked essence, bringing a taste of fire to the ocean.'

PAUL CHUNG - SAISON HOSPITALITY

California Urchin Gimmari.

SERVES 40

FOR THE RICE

340g California Koshihikari rice
350g filtered water
6g sea mustard (miyeok), in large strips and dried
3g maesaengi seaweed (Capsosiphon fulvescens), fresh, cut into 1cm pieces
OR
1g maesaengi seaweed (Capsosiphon fulvescens), freeze-dried
29g mirin
28g Akazu vinegar
42g aged cultured butter

Measure out the rice into a large stainless-stell mixing bowl. Cover with cold filtered water and agitate gently until the water turns cloudy. Strain through a fine-mesh colander. Place back into the mixing bowl and repeat the process 3 more times.
After the fourth time, return the rice to the mixing bowl and cover with cold filtered water and allow to soak undisturbed for 5 minutes. Strain through a colander and allow to drain undisturbed for 15 minutes. Combine the rice with the measured filtered water in a rice cooker, then place the dried *miyeok* and fresh *maesaengi* on top. Cook the rice on the sushi rice setting. Once the rice is cooked, allow to rest for 15 minutes. Once the rice is rested, transfer the rice to a large bowl. Remove the *miyeok* and gently fold in the mirin, vinegar and butter. Once everything is thoroughly mixed, return the rice to the rice cooker and keep at the warm setting.

FOR THE URCHINS

8-10 whole red urchins, 40 urchin tongues, fresh, grade A, large smoked tuna garum, as required
2 California kelp leaves, smoked and dried

Using a fishbone tweezer, gently break and peel off the urchin shell starting from the mouth. Continue in a circular motion, making sure not to break or tear the gonads of the urchin. Continue until one-third of the shell has been removed, and the gonads are protruding above the rim of the shell. Using a palette knife, pry the gonads gently from the remaining shell into a bowl of ice water.
Wash the urchin to remove any residual veins, then gently pat them dry before placing them on the smoked and dried kelp. Spray the urchin with tuna garum to season, then gently place another piece of kelp on top. Store in the refrigerator for 20 minutes before removing the urchin from the kelp and reserving for later use.

FOR THE PRESERVED URCHINS

450g red urchin gonads, grade A, imperfect trim
100g tamari smoked with almond wood
9g fine sea salt
almond wood

Gently place the urchin in a stainless-steel bowl and pour the smoked tamari over. Allow the urchin to rest in the tamari for 1 hour. Remove the urchin and place on a linen towel to absorb the residual tamari.
Dust with the salt then roll the urchin into a cylinder shape using plastic wrap. Ensure that it is not too tight or it will 'pop' the urchin.

Poke holes through the plastic, so that the urchin can breathe and dry out. Hang the urchin in the dry-ageing cabinet at 41 °C (106 °F) and at 75% RH for 2–3 weeks. You will need to unwrap and rewrap the urchin multiple times as it dehydrates and shrinks in size.

Once it is 80% dried, wrap the urchin in a single layer of cheesecloth and hang next an almond wood fire, allowing the smoke and gentle heat to finish off the drying and ageing process,

Once finished, the urchin should be firm and compressed into a single piece. Blast-chill, then store in the freezer.

FOR THE GAMTAE

gamtae, *cut into 3.2cm x 20.3cm strips*

Combine both ingredients in a CRYOVAC bag and fully compress,

FOR THE EGG YOLK GLAZE

110g organic egg yolks from pasture-raised hens
25g smoked tamari

TO PLATE

Take a small handful of rice (roughly 25g) and shape it into an oblong. Wrap in the *gamtae*, then push down into the rice to create a slight pocket or divot.

Place the *gimmari* (Korean term for things wrapped in seaweeds) in the smoker for 1 minute to fully warm through.

Place one large piece of urchin into the divot, and glaze with the egg yolk mixture. Squeeze 3 drops of yuzu on top. Shave a good amount of the aged urchin and place on top. Serve immediately. This is best eaten with your hands and in just a couple of bites!

Mauro Colagreco.

MIRAZUR, MENTON (FR)

Born in 1976 in La Plata, Argentina, Mauro Colagreco moved to France to work with Bernard Loiseau, Alain Passard and Alain Ducasse. In 2006, the chef opened Mirazur in Menton on the French Riviera, and gained his first Michelin star less than a year later. Now with three stars on his chef's hat, crowned The Best Restaurant in the World in 2019, Colagreco is committed to circular gastronomy and respect for nature's cycle, with Mirazur's gardens setting the pace in the kitchen.

✕ What is your signature dish?

MAURO COLAGRECO: *Our way of working at Mirazur has always been to use the ingredients available in our gardens and in our region. That's why we offer our guests a surprise menu, an experience designed to discover our terroir. The menu follows the rhythm of our gardens from day to day. It is a menu of 365 seasons, in constant evolution, where each dish can be different from one day to the next. After the Covid lockdowns, we began to propose a menu more closely related to the biodynamic work we do in our gardens, which offers four variations: Root, Leaf, Flower and Fruit.*

So, rather than talking about signature dishes, we could talk about signature ingredients. We have dishes that are more famous than others and are linked to a particular history, to our philosophy and to our commitments, such as caviar beet, Naranjo en Flor, Black Tide, Squid and Bagna Cauda Sauce.

✕ What does your signature dish tell us about you?

MAURO COLAGRECO: *This dish is an invitation to redefine the meaning of luxury. It presents one of the poorest ingredients of the agricultural tradition, the beet, accompanied by one of the most luxurious*

ingredients, caviar. This becomes a revelation because all the richness of this dish lies in the 'know-how' of the vegetable in the making, first its cultivation and then its preparation. The beet is being transformed all the way through to its final state, creating the element of real "preciousness". In this way, the dish embodies our philosophy because our most precious work is made together with nature, which gives rhythm and tone to our cuisine.

× **What is the story behind its creation?**

MAURO COLAGRECO: *I was inspired by the work of Annie Bertin who has been cultivating produce at her own farm in the North of France since 1992. She has been very generous in sharing her knowledge with me. Her work combines creativity and observational techniques to reveal the rhythms of nature at a deeper level. On her farm, the produce is the centre of attention and is respected and perceived as a work of art.*

Another great source of inspiration is the work and philosophy of Masanobu Fukuoka, the father of permaculture. It's based on the awareness built around observation and listening to the forces at work in nature.

× **What type of beet is used for this dish?**

MAURO COLAGRECO: *This dish is made with crapaudine beet, which has been cultivated over an entire year. Once harvested, it's stored in a cellar all winter under a cover of straw. The beet is then replanted the following year in order to mature it to a maximum for another year. In this way, it concentrates all the aromas and sugar. We then cook it like meat using one of the oldest techniques: coated with salt. Through these production and cooking techniques, we transform this simple ingredient into the most luxurious one.*

× **How would you describe your cuisine and the philosophy behind it?**

MAURO COLAGRECO: *My cuisine is guided and inspired by nature and by the love I have for the region I live in and am still discovering every day. It's an evolving cuisine, heavily based on vegetables, which follows the seasons and is punctuated by the cycles of the moon. I allow myself to follow my intuitions and call upon all the influences that have marked me and that continue to surprise me with a single premise: respect for the produce, of sublimation of nature.*

× **How and when did you become passionate about food?**

MAURO COLAGRECO: *I come from a family that loves to celebrate and share around the table. I am the first one to cook professionally, but in my family, everyone loves to cook and enjoy good food. After four years of studying economics and paying for my tuition, I started working at a friend's restaurant. I immediately loved the atmosphere of the kitchens, the creative agitation, the effervescence... I discovered that I love this profession.*

× **What are the characteristics of the dishes you like to cook?**

MAURO COLAGRECO: *Dishes that surprise our senses. Colourful, fragrant and with contrasts that invite full harmony. In fact, for me, a good dish is one where the chef succeeds to 'step aside' and brings to the forefront the wonder of nature's good ingredients — a dish that can communicate an emotion rather than a gesture.*

× **What are your three favourite ingredients?**

MAURO COLAGRECO: *It's difficult to answer due to the richness of the ingredients we have in our region, but I would like to suggest three: the tomato, and the generosity of its varieties; the seaweed, which brings umami to our dashi and our preparations; and the candied lemon — I am in Menton, the city of lemons and they are magnificent!*

MAURO COLAGRECO - MIRAZUR

Beetroot caviar.

SERVES 6 – 8

FOR THE BEETROOT

1 crapaudine beetroot
2kg Guérande grey sea salt
30g water

Mix the salt and water in a mixing bowl. Arrange a thin layer of the moistened salt over a gastro plate covered with parchment paper. Arrange the beetroot over the middle of the plate and cover completely with the rest of the salt.
Cook the beetroot for 3 hours at 180 °C (355 °F) until dry. Then remove the beetroot pieces from the salt crust, peeling off any salt that has stuck to the beetroot pieces.
Using a ham slicer, cut the beetroot into fairly thin slices. Keep them between two sheets of baking paper until the rest of the recipe is completed.

FOR THE SAUCE

40g Oscietra caviar (5–7g per person)
80g pouring cream (35% fat)

Pour the cold cream into a mixing bowl and mix gently with the caviar until you have a homogeneous mixture. There should be approx. 10g of cream and 5g of caviar for each portion.

TO PLATE

Arrange three or four beautiful slices of beet in a hollow plate, creating as much volume as possible. Top with two spoonfuls of the sauce.

Alexandre Couillon.

LA MARINE, NOIRMOUTIER (FR)

Born in 1975, French chef Alexandre Couillon took over his parents' ailing restaurant, La Marine, on the island of Noirmoutier in Brittany. With the help of his wife Céline, the chef has transformed it into a gourmet destination worth missing the last ferry for.

—— In 1999, Alexandre and Céline Couillon took over La Marine, 'like two enthusiastic kids, a little oblivious', as Couillon remembers. They didn't yet know it, but the husband-and-wife team was about to turn a simple moules-frites family restaurant in the little fishing port of L'Herbaudière into one of the most sought-after culinary hotspots in France. However, that same year, disaster struck the small island of Noirmoutier. On 12 December, the oil tanker Erika sank off the coast of Brittany, releasing 31,000 tonnes of heavy fuel oil, killing marine life and contaminating the waters and French coast for over 400 km, from Finistère to Charente-Maritime. It was an unprecedented disaster for the region.

'Everything was soiled,' remembers Alexandre Couillon. 'The rocks, the fish. The birds were dying on the beach. Once the service at the restaurant finished, we joined the volunteers to clean up the oily waste. It was painstaking work.' Yet out of this disaster came beauty, in the form of this oyster dish, also known as the Erika oyster.

'The birth of a dish is a mystery. The Erika oyster, now inseparable from La Marine on Noirmoutier, was inspired by an ecological disaster,' sums up Couillon, who recalls its creation a few years later, in 2013: 'Years had passed and La Marine had just won its second star. We were on cloud nine. I was working on a squid-based jus. It was all back and very beautiful, but not a colour associated with food. I had a flash of inspiration: Why can't I make a dish out of it? A black spot on a white plate.'

And so 'chaos has given birth to a star', a dish of black oyster poached in Colonnata lard with squid made with a thick oyster that is grown specially for La Marine, and then poached in an iodised broth. On the surface, 'the powderised Colonnata lard brings to mind limestone, while a sugar pastille recalls a fragment of mother-of-pearl, silver and crystalline.' Finally the sweetness of the squid ink jus softens the iodine. 'It's daring, but it works. It's perhaps my most personal dish; it's impossible to take it off the menu. Who knows, maybe one day I will add Covid scallops to my repertoire...'

ALEXANDRE COUILLON - LA MARINE

Oysters with lardo and squid bouillon.

SERVES 4

FOR THE TAPIOCA PEARLS

30g tapioca
150ml water
200ml lemon juice
40ml oyster juice
15g cuttlefish ink paste
15g caster sugar

Simmer the tapioca pearls in water for about 10 minutes. Add the lemon juice and the oyster juice. Mix and add the cuttlefish ink and the sugar. Reheat for 10 minutes and set aside in a cool place.

FOR THE SQUID BOUILLON

60g lardo di Colonnata
50g leeks
50g onions
1kg fresh ungutted squid
1.5L mineral water
10g cuttlefish ink paste
2 gas cartridges

Brown the *lardo*. Add the thinly sliced leeks and onions and sauté without browning. Add the whole squid, then add the water. Simmer slowly for about 1 hour. Add the cuttlefish ink. Strain and refrigerate. Pour into a syphon and add the gas cartridges.

FOR THE OYSTERS

4 large no. 1 oysters

Open the oysters and rinse well to remove any pieces of shell. Place in a vacuum bag and add the syphon of bouillon. Cook in an immersion heater at 55 °C (131 °F) for 2 minutes. Chill in a basin of iced water for 1 hour.

FOR THE LARDO FOAM

100g lardo di Colonnata
malt powder

Melt the *lardo* and beat to a foam with the malt powder.

FOR THE SUGAR PASTILLES

50g isomalt
edible silver powder

Melt the isomalt with a touch of silver powder. Drop a spot of this hot mixture on a stainless-steel work surface. Crush with the base of a small saucepan and quickly unstick the pastille using the blade of a knife.

TO PLATE

20g crystallised ginger, dried and powdered
edible silver powder

Place an oyster in the centre of a plate. Add a few tapioca pearls, a little powdered crystallised ginger, silver powder and *lardo* foam, plus a sugar pastille.

Sang Hoon Degeimbre.

L'AIR DU TEMPS, LIERNU (BE)

Born in South Korea and adopted by a Belgian family, self-taught chef Sang Hoon Degeimbre was a sommelier before opening his first restaurant, L'Air du Temps, in 2000 with his ex-wife Carine. It now has two Michelin stars, a 5 hectares organic garden, and is a pioneer in sustainability in the region.

—— 'I have many signature dishes, says Degeimbre, 'but one of my favourites is Jardins de Liernu (often shortened to Liernu), after the name of the village where the restaurant is based.' The vegetarian dish, composed of seasonal vegetables sublimated by fermented jus and green oil, comes straight from the restaurant's extensive kitchen garden, managed by Degeimbre's friend and partner Benoît Blairvacq.

'This signature dish is always the same but never the same… like me,' says the chef. 'I am always in motion and everything depends on the mood, the season or the envy. It's an all-year-long à la carte dish that keeps changing. It's also a tribute to the garden, the earth, the human and nature. I can't say exactly what the ingredients will be.'

The dish is 'simple but complex, comfortable but pushy,' and despite the seasonal changes, always features a handful of vegetables at their best, cooked or raw, served with fermented vegetable juice, farm butter and green oil. 'At the beginning of the year, it's more about fermented products and wild herbs from fields or forests,' explains Degeimbre.
'Sometimes we focus on one vegetable such as radish or turnip. And during summer, it's made of more than 20 different greens or fruits. It surprises you every time, that's the idea.'

A self-described 'citizen of the world' now at the forefront of Belgian gastronomy, Degeimbre says his success lies both in the freshness of his ingredients and in his close network of craftspeople, riders and providers. 'My cooking style depends on the humans involved, their passion and talent.' His own passion was honed from a young age and keeps on growing. 'I've realised that I'm a little more passionate with each passing day. I wanted to understand the backstage of cooking, which is why I have always been interested in physical and chemical reactions in the kitchen,' says the chef, who has attended courses given by the French scientist Hervé This, the inventor of molecular gastronomy', adds the chef.

Now with a strong brigade and a team of four full-time gardeners tending to a kitchen garden planted with over 400 varieties of edible plants, L'Air du Temps focuses on its ecological approach and its politics of zero organic waste to create unexpected dishes with 'a pinch of creativity and honesty.'

SANG HOON DEGEIMBRE - L'AIR DU TEMPS

Les Jardins de Liernu.

Seasonal vegetables, lacto-fermented juice and lovage oil. Herbs and flowers. Mole salsa.

SERVES 1

FOR THE JARDINS DE LIERNU

3 rings of leek
3 bevelled slices of radish
3 thin slices of kohlrabi
3 bevelled slices of carrot
3 bevelled slices of asparagus
3 thin slices of pickle
3 thin slices of fermented beetroot
3 fava beans
3 chive flowers
3 red hot lips flowers
3 bronze oregano leaves
3 pieces of fennel fronds
3 nettle leaves

Clean the leek, radish, carrot (with peel) and asparagus. Clean the flowers and herbs.
Blanch the leek and separate the layers, keeping them entire. Slice 1 layer into 2cm 'rings'.
Cut the radish into 8 bevelled slices lengthwise.
Peel the kohlrabi and cut it into thin slices using a mandoline.
Cook the small carrots with the peel on. Allow to cool and peel by hand.
Cut each carrot into eighths lengthwise.
Blanch the asparagus for 1 minute. Cut into eighths lengthwise.
Cut the pickle into thin slices.
Smoke the fermented beetroot. Cut into thin slices.
Fry the nettle leaves.
Reserve three pieces/slices/leaves of each vegetable, flower and herb.

FOR THE *CROUSTILLANT* OF BEETROOT

200g smashed potatoes
100g beetroot juice
30g isomalt
3g konjac

Peal, clean, boil and drain the potatoes. Mix them with the beetroot juice, the isomalt and the konjac. Mix at 80 °C (175 °F).
Spread thinly and bake in the oven at 90 °C (195 °F) for 30 minutes. Finish in the dehydrator at 55 °C (130 °F).

FOR THE 'LACTO' JUICE

200g pickle juice
30g shallots
60g butter
salt, to taste
lemon juice, to taste
lovage oil
150g grapeseed oil
100g lovage
2g salt

Reduce the pickle juice with the chopped shallots. Strain and add the butter (up to 50% of the liquid). Add salt and lemon juice to taste.

FOR THE *SALADINE*

15 oxalis flowers
5 pieces of dill

FOR THE MOLE SALSA
MAKES 600G

200g lacto-fermented peppers
200g tamari (Japanese soy sauce)
10g grapeseed oil
70g onion
30g garlic
5g ground black pepper
20g tomato paste
400g green jangajji tomatoes
5g smoked paprika
100g coriander
20g cocoa paste
5g cinnamon
salt, if needed

Cut and deseed the lacto-fermented peppers.
Cut and deseed the green jangajji tomatoes.
Brown the onion and garlic in the oil, then add the tomato paste. Next add the peppers and tomatoes, and finish with the tamari. Cook everything covered on a low heat for 2 hours.
Season with pepper, paprika, cocoa paste and cinnamon. Cook again for 1 hour, then finish in a food processor to achieve a smooth texture, adding the fresh coriander. Adjust the seasoning with salt if needed.

TO PLATE

Place every slice, leaf or roll of vegetable as well as the *croustillant* using the picture as a model. Carefully pour the lacto-fermented juice around the vegetables. Add some delicate drops of lovage oil to the juice together with dabs of the mole salsa. Finish with the oxalis flowers and dill as decoration.

Richard Ekkebus.

AMBER, HONG KONG (CN)

Originally from the Netherlands, Richard Ekkebus is the executive chef of the Mandarin Oriental Landmark Hotel in Hong Kong and its fine-dining restaurant, Amber, celebrating consciously sourced ingredients and French techniques. It was awarded two Michelin stars in December 2008.

—— Richard Ekkebus's Aka Uni dish was originally created in 2006, at a time when sea urchins were not widely used in French restaurants. 'It's a dish that made an unapproachable ingredient approachable,' says the classically trained chef, who has worked for the likes of Hans Snijders, Robert Kranenborg, Guy Savoy and Pierre Gagnaire. 'I think the dish showcases my personality as someone who is willing to take up a challenge. I like to work with less approachable ingredients from sustainable sources.'

Featuring a Hokkaido sea urchin in a jacket of lobster jelly atop a bed of cauliflower cream, the dish was removed from Amber's menu in 2015, and 'donated' to the San Francisco MOMA restaurant as a creation. This created quite a stir in the local foodie community, and the dish eventually returned to Amber in 2018. It was reinvented a year later, when Amber reopened with a focus on sustainable dining and vegetarian dishes.

'It became a challenge to create a new version of the sea urchin dish as it was curated out of butter, milk and cream,' explains Ekkebus. 'In the new recipe, we have replaced the original ingredients with plant-based ones, such as almond milk, coconut fat and enriched soy to keep its creamy indulgent texture. The sea umami flavours also stand out without the animal fats, where the flavours of the whole dish become cleaner. The dish also signified Amber's transformation and how we gave this signature dish a "second life".'

Ekkebus is keen to source only ethical ingredients from sustainable sources. 'At Amber 2.0, we use no dairy, very little salt, no refined flours and sugars, and we aim for 75% plant-based proteins and 25% animal proteins in our menus. These are limitations that we set for ourselves and that push us to be creative. Limitations drive creativity.'

RICHARD EKKEBUS - AMBER

Aka Uni cauliflower, lobster and Daurenki Tsar Impérial caviar.

SERVES 30

FOR THE CAULIFLOWER PURÉE

500g cauliflower, chopped
50g pure virgin coconut cooking butter
1L unsweetened soy milk
salt, to taste

Sweat the cauliflower in the coconut butter and season with salt. Cover with soy milk, cover with a lid, and cook until very soft. Strain, then blend until smooth, adding some of the cooking liquid if required. Pass and check the seasoning.

FOR THE CAULIFLOWER MOUSSE

400g cauliflower purée
800g whipped enriched soy cream
2 leaves of gelatine, soaked and dissolved

Warm the purée, add the gelatine and mix. Put into a bowl over iced water and mix until cold. Fold in the soy cream and lightly season with salt.

FOR THE LOBSTER JELLY

1L lobster consommé
6 leaves of gelatine, soaked

Warm the consommé, add the gelatine, dissolve and pass.

FOR THE TAPIOCA TUILLE

400g tapioca flour
3L water
40g seaweed powder

Whisk the flour and water, put on the stove, and bring to the boil, whisking continuously until the mix goes clear, then cook over a low heat for 30 minutes.
Remove from the stove, season with salt and whisk in the seaweed powder. Divide between 6 trays and spread over a Silpat-covered tray in a thin, even layer (as thin as possible). Put into a dry oven at 65 °C (150 °F) and leave overnight. Remove from the oven and store in sealed bags.
Deep-fry in sunflower oil at 180–190 °C (355–375 °F) and season lightly with salt.

TO FINISH AND PLATE PER SERVING

30g sea urchin
cauliflower mousse
lobster jelly
15g Daurenki Tsar Impérial caviar
gold leaf
1 tapioca tuile

With a small, pointed pair of scissors, open the sea urchins at the top and open so they each form a perfect circle, then rinse under running water to remove the black membrane and intestines. Upend the urchins on a towel to remove all excess water. Using a small teaspoon, scoop out the 5 tongues from each shell. Clean the urchin shells and store in the refrigerator for later use. Use a small ramekin of 5cm diameter. Cool them down prior to plating. Select the 90 best, most perfect-looking sea urchin tongues and set aside. For each serving, place a couple of the less nice tongues in the centre of the cooled urchin shells, cover with the cauliflower mousse in a dome shape, then place 3 perfect tongues neatly on the cauliflower mousse.

Put the shells in the refrigerator for 1 hour to set. After they have set, cover each with 2 tablespoons of the almost-set lobster jelly, then place in the refrigerator for another 1 hour to set.

Use a half-dome mould (the equivalent of a US tablespoon measure) to shape the caviar domes. Place the dome centrally on top of the lobster jelly and finish with gold leaf. Serve the tapioca tuile to one side.

Adeline Grattard.

YAM'TCHA, PARIS (FR)

Born in 1978 in Dijon, Adeline Grattard is the head chef of the Michelin-starred French-Asian restaurant Yam'Tcha in the centre of Paris, which she opened with her Hong Kong-born husband Chi Wah Chan in 2009.

—— Originally from Burgundy, Grattard worked under Pascal Barbot at L'Astrance in Paris before following her tea specialist husband back to his native Hong Kong for a couple of years. But her signature dish of poulpe des îles has even more exotic origins, recalling the paradisiacal islands of the Seychelles rather than the skyscrapers of her adopted home.

Grattard had the opportunity to travel a lot with her parents, which increased her fascination for exotic cuisine — she once said she dreamt of ginger and chilli as a child. 'Before I left France to live in Hong Kong, our parents took my sister and me to the Seychelles for ten days,' the chef explains. 'On the island of La Digue, which was very wild at the time, we sunbathed on the white sand with a beach shack behind us, crammed full of local specialities. That's why this famous octopus dish will forever remain engraved in our minds. This dish is locally called zurit and the Seychellois are wild about it. To tenderise the octopus, they bang them on the rocks between the white sand and the coconut palms.'

The dish became such a hit with Grattard's family that it became part of their Christmas repertoire. 'This recipe is entirely based on the memory of the taste,' says Grattard, 'which is not difficult when you have succumbed to the delights of this famous dish every day for ten whole days!' The Colombo and coconut curry might make an appearance on Yam'Tcha's ever-changing menu, which includes dishes such as Stilton bao with Amarena cherries and sweet-and-sour prawns with star fruit and pomegranate.

But it's highly unlikely that you will be lucky enough to order it, as Grattard's offering is constantly in flux, depending on market finds and the inspiration of the moment. Repeat customers have said that they have never come across the same dish twice, except perhaps for the baos, so your guess is as good as ours as to what you will find there. 'My cooking focuses on the quality of the products, on feeling and the intensity of the moment,' says Grattard. 'I best enjoy cooking to make people happy.'

ADELINE GRATTARD - YAM'TCHA

Island octopus.

SERVES 4 (MAIN DISH) OR 6 (STARTER)

FOR THE OCTOPUS

1 octopus, weight 1kg
100g coarse sea salt

Wash the octopus by rubbing it lightly with the coarse salt and kneading it in the sink to tenderise it, and rinse well in clean water. Remove the contents of the head and separate the tentacles. Place in a steamer basket and steam for 45 minutes. It should be tender if you prick it with a knife. Leave to cool, then cut into strips.

FOR THE SAUCE

1 garlic clove, finely chopped
1 shallot, finely chopped
1 red pepper, finely chopped
1 piece of ginger, finely chopped
1 tsp Colombo curry powder
1 tsp olive oil
1 tsp tomato concentrate
4 kaffir lime (combava) leaves
500ml coconut milk
black pepper and fleur de sel

Sauté the garlic, shallot, ginger and red pepper in the olive oil, together with the Colombo curry powder, until soft. Add the tomato concentrate, cook for a few minutes, and add the coconut milk. Bring to a simmer, add the octopus strips and cook over low heat for 5 minutes.
Add the kaffir lime leaves. Season with pepper and *fleur de sel*. Then leave to cool and eat the following day.

Mehmet Gürs.

MIKLA, ISTANBUL (TR)

Born in 1973, Mehmet Gürs is a celebrated Finnish-Turkish chef based in Istanbul, where he honours his region through new Anatolian cuisine at his restaurant Mikla since 2005.

—— Fittingly for a bi-national chef, Mehmet Gürs's signature dish is from the Bosphorus Strait, which marks the geographical boundary between Europe and Asia. Called balık ekmek, or fish bread, the dish was created in 2005.

'This is the street name for the grilled fish sandwich that has been sold on the shores of the Bosphorus and the Golden Horn for decades,' explains Gürs. 'I remember it being good when I visited Istanbul as a kid, but then when I moved there in 1996, it was almost impossible to find a good one. Most of these sandwiches were made using frozen fish from Norway and poor quality bread.'

Gürs's take on the humble fish sandwich features hamsi, or Black Sea anchovy. 'It's one of my favourite fish of the region; when in season it's tasty, healthy, abundant and cheap,' says the chef. 'I messed around in the kitchen to see what I could do with it. There are many traditional ways of preparing it, and as with many other dishes in the region, the traditionalists don't like it. The result of my playing around was a really super tasty, fatty, crispy bite-sized "sandwich".'

The other element of the dish is slightly more unusual – and one we wouldn't recommend biting into. 'On one of my trips to the Anatolian countryside, I drove by an enormous hydroelectric plant and saw the mass destruction that it had caused,' continues Gürs. 'Standing in a dry river bed in the mountainous eastern Black Sea region, thinking of all the life that had been there before brought tears to my eyes. It was like a scene from the film *Mad Max*. Pure destruction. I took with me a few beautiful smooth pebbles from the dead river where once life was abundant. Back in Istanbul, I made a slit in the pebbles with an angle grinder.'

The result is a striking dish that highlights both the destruction of the environment, and Gürs's activism and commitment to a better, more sustainable future. '"Dead fish in a stone from a dead river," or as we call it, "balık ekmek".'

MEHMET GÜRS - MIKLA

Balık ekmek. *(fried hamsi sandwich)*

SERVES 1

FOR THE OLIVE OIL BREAD
MAKES 100 PIECES

1.5kg all-purpose flour
70g fresh yeast
150g extra-virgin olive oil
30g sea salt
800g water, lukewarm

Add the yeast to the lukewarm water and mix well. Add the salt and 50g of the olive oil. Sift the flour in and knead until smooth.
Place the dough into a deep half-size (15 cm) Gastropan. Spread out evenly in the pan. Brush liberally with the remaining olive oil (100g). Cover and allow to rise for 20 minutes.
Bake in a preheated static oven at 200 °C (390 °F) for 40 minutes. Remove from pan and allow to rest overnight
Thinly slice the bread (8mm), and cut each slice into 9 x 4.5 cm rectangles. Cover until use.

FOR THE LEMON MAYONNAISE
MAKES 400G

2 eggs
1 egg yolk
60g lemon juice
salt
white pepper
250g light olive oil
80g extra-virgin olive oil

Add the eggs, egg yolk and half of the lemon juice to a mixer and whip on a medium speed. Next add the salt, pepper and remaining lemon juice and mix a little more. Now slowly add both oils while continuing to mix, Transfer the mixture into an ISI syphon. Load with 2 cartridges and keep cool until use.
Use at room temperature.

TO PLATE
FOR 1 PORTION

1 hamsi anchovy fillet, cleaned, skin on
1 rectangle of olive oil bread
5g butter, clarified
5g lemon mayonnaise
chives, chopped

Place the sliced olive oil bread on a piece of baking paper. Season the anchovy fillet with sea salt and black pepper. Place on the bread skin down and lightly press down so that it sticks. Wrap and rest it in the cooler for 4 hours, so that the anchovy fillet sticks well and truly to the bread.
Place a non-stick pan over medium heat, and add the butter. Place the fish sandwich bread side down in the pan and fry until the bread is golden brown and crispy. Cook on one side only.
Pipe the lemon mayonnaise in a ramekin, add some finely chopped chives and serve on the side of the fried hamsi sandwich.

Brian Mark Hansen.

SØLLERØD KRO, COPENHAGEN (DK)

Leading Danish chef Brian Mark Hansen was born in Vojens in 1982. He became head chef at the Michelin-starred Søllerød Kro in 2013. Located right outside of Copenhagen, the 330-year-old restaurant offers a remarkable food experience, enhanced by its restaurant manager Jan Restorff and its team.

—— Hailing from southern Denmark, Brian Mark Hansen grew up in Vojens, where his parents owned the local inn. He spent his childhood helping them in the kitchen ('My gastronomic journey began as a child in my parents' house,' he says), before starting his career at Ruths Hotel in Skagen, under Michel Michaud, a French chef who brought French cuisine to Denmark in 1971; and Kong Hans Kælder, Copenhagen's first French-style gourmet restaurant.

Hansen's lemon sole dish, which is topped with caviar, features key ingredients from his native region. 'Where I am from in the south of Denmark, on the border with Germany, we eat a lot of fish and cabbage,' the chef explains. 'But despite the simple appearance of my signature dish, it has a complex, deep flavour with nerve and edge.'

Hansen describes his style of cooking as an exercise in simplicity: 'My philosophy is to not make it complicated, to keep the pure taste and follow the seasons and your own terroir.' His cuisine has a solid French base and Nordic roots, while his creations are decidedly contemporary and include dishes such as scallop, dashi, yuzu and white soya, as well as a Christian Andersen-themed children's menu that won him the 2023 Bocuse d'Or.

Among his main influences are the natural world, French cuisine and the work of Thomas Keller, the American chef who founded The French Laundry in Napa Valley, while his favourite cooking ingredients are truffle, onion and fish, especially the turbot found in Danish waters, which he says is the best in the world.

'Respect for tradition is the most important thing to me,' the chef says. It's no wonder he has chosen Søllerød Kro, a three-century old thatched inn outside Copenhagen, as his base. It's a welcome alternative to the capital's trendy New Nordic Cuisine, which has been rewarded year after year for its excellence in preparing everything from venison to pork and lobster.

BRIAN MARK HANSEN - SØLLERØD KRO

Lemon sole with fermented daikon sauce, parsley and Ossetra caviar.

SERVES 10

FOR THE DAIKON BROTH

1kg daikon (mooli) radish
15g kombu seaweed
1L brine (2.2%)

Cut the daikon into thin strips and mixed with the brine. Store in a fermentation jar in a cool (around 29 °C or 84.2 °F) dark place for about 3–5 weeks until the brine has a rich flavour. Sieve the broth and reserve for the sauce.

FOR THE FINISHED SAUCE

150g fermented daikon broth
50g blue mussel stock
75g Danish butter
15g peanut oil

Whisk all the ingredients together to create a smooth sauce. Split with parsley chlorophyll.

FOR THE PARSLEY CHLOROPHYLL

300g broad-leaved parsley
100g spinach
500g oil

Cook and blend in a saucepan to 70 °C (158 °F) then pass through a sieve.

FOR THE LEMON SOLE

Fillet the lemon sole and salt for 8 minutes in a salt and sugar solution (40-salt-10g sugar-1L water).
Cut and temper at 44 °C (111.2 °F).

TO PLATE

Add Royal Oscietra Belgium Caviar without borax in abundant quantities.

Zaiyu Hasegawa.

DEN, TOKYO (JP)

Born in Tokyo in 1978, Zaiyu Hasegawa opened Den in 2007 and is known for his playful and creative dishes. Voted Asia's Best Restaurant 2022, Den has two Michelin stars and its mascot is Pucci Jr, a Chihuahua.

— 'I want to cook food that makes people smile. And I want them to want to come back again,' says Zaiyu Hasegawa, the friendly head chef at Den in Tokyo, whose signature dish is 'the DFC, a deep-fried chicken wing stuffed with sticky rice and seasonal ingredients.'

It's part of a kaiseki meal, a traditional multi-course Japanese dinner. 'Kaiseki originated from the tea ceremony in which a very strong matcha would be served, and it has evolved into drinking sake and wine with a meal,' explains Hasegawa. 'If you have strong matcha or alcohol on an empty stomach, it is not good for you. The DFC corresponds to the oshinogi course of the meal, a course served quite early on, to prepare your stomach for it. It is usually composed of a small portion of rice, or soba, or something relatively substantial.'

When Den first opened, Hasegawa served seasonal oshinogi, but soon wondered how he could make it tastier and more enjoyable. 'That's why we created Den-tucky. We thought guests would enjoy opening the DFC box and eating the casual dish with their hands if they were uncomfortable with chopsticks.'

Hasegawa puts his guest first, always: 'I cook with the other person in mind, with love and from the heart. He says he became a chef because he loved the food his parents cooked for him as a child; his mother was a geisha who worked in a *ryotei* (traditional high-end restaurant), which explains his early interest in Japanese cooking.

Hasegawa prefers 'local food and soul food — that the Japanese like to eat — to fine dining.' The chef loves inventing dishes using mushrooms, rice and fish that are from the wild and natural environment of Japan, and he cites the late Japanese chef Mari Hirata for having greatly influenced his work.

ZAIYU HASEGAWA - DEN

DFC. *(Den fried chicken)*

SERVES 18 (MAIN DISH) OR 35 (STARTER)

FOR THE CHICKEN WINGS

wings of freshly slaughtered chickens
flour for dredging
oil for deep-frying

Debone the wing, make a pocket (where the bones used to be) and stuff with one of the fillings given below and seal the opening with a toothpick. Sprinkle with salt and rest for 1.5–2 hours to drain excess moisture from the chicken.
Dredge the chicken dumpling in flour and deep-fry in oil at 180 °C (356 °F). Drain off any excess oil and lightly sear under a salamander, then serve while still hot and crispy.

Here are two different stuffing recipes:

FOR STUFFING 1

Sticky black rice flavoured with *yakuzen* (Chinese medicinal) ingredients

(ENOUGH FOR ABOUT 35 DUMPLINGS)

180g black rice
180g sticky rice
50g ginseng
120ml sake
salt
50g pine nuts, toasted
70g goji wolfberries
juice of grated ginger

Mix the black rice and sticky rice in a bowl, and soak in water overnight. Drain in a strainer.
Chop the ginseng finely and soak in the sake. Wrap the rice in Sarashi cotton cloth and steam for 15 minutes.
Sprinkle the ginseng with sake and salt on the rice and steam for another 15 minutes.
Mix the pine nuts, the wolfberries (rinsed in sake) and the juice of grated ginger juice with the steamed rice.

FOR STUFFING 2

Spicy sticky rice with almond

(ENOUGH FOR ABOUT
18 CHICKEN WINGS)

180g steamed sticky rice
50g roasted almonds
50g raisins
3g mixture of cumin and
garam masala

Add the almond, raisins and mixed spices to the steamed sticky rice.

Sergio Herman.

LE PRISTINE, ANTWERP (BE)

Known for his love for Zeeland products, the Dutch chef and entrepreneur Sergio Herman was born in 1970 in Oostburg. His restaurants include Pure C, Air Café, Blueness and Le Pristine, which he opened in Antwerp in 2020.

— It's no surprise that Sergio Herman chose the humble bivalve as the star ingredient of his signature dish of mussels a la marinera. Herman began his career in his teens in his family's mussel restaurant Oud Sluis in Sluis, and transformed it into a top gastronomic destination with three Michelin stars before shutting it down in 2013, not before it was immortalised in a documentary titled *Sergio Herman – F*cking Perfect*. His love for mussels even extends to writing an entire cookbook dedicated to the 'black gold'.

'When I was 14, I helped in the kitchen. I had to stack the burlap sacks — which weighed up to 20 kilos — in the refrigerator. Every day 15 to 20 bags were delivered. That's a few hundred kilos I had to lift,' the chef once revealed. 'In addition, every day I had to peel onions and wash and cut celery and parsley. And then there was the mussel sauce: I made litres! I had a real love-hate relationship with mussels.' And that's without mentioning the smell of mussels, which permeated our family's upstairs living room.'

Herman is a celebrity in Belgium and the Netherlands, thanks to his appearances as a stern mentor in TV cooking shows, his gourmet empire of star-rated and fine-dining restaurants in Belgium and the Netherlands, and his premium fast-food brand, Frites Atelier. But for this signature dish featuring a marinara tomato sauce, the chef looks further out, reminiscing about holidays in the sun, on a party-loving Mediterranean island: 'This dish is so simple,' he says. 'It's a reference to a plate full of happiness with the flavours of Ibiza. Eating this dish in the late afternoon on the beach with your family or friends, as you relax and enjoy the sunset and *sobremesa*, brings tears of happiness.'

'There's more than mussels in white wine,' Herman has said – although he still thinks his dad's original, creamy white wine recipe is the best. At the Italian-inspired Le Pristine, mussels are paired with gnocchi, nduja and artichoke, or are flavoured with fresh lovage and savoury pecorino.

SERGIO HERMAN - LE PRISTINE

Mussels with marinera sauce.

SERVES 2

FOR THE MARINERA SAUCE

6 shallots
1 garlic glove
500g tomatoes from a jar (preferably Italian)
80g olive oil
10g basil leaves

Add the chopped shallots, the finely chopped garlic and olive oil to a pan, together with a pinch of salt, and cook for few minutes on a medium heat until soft but without any colour.
Add the tomatoes and simmer for 10 minutes. Add the basil leaves and cook for a couple more minutes. Pass through a fine sieve, then reduce to achieve the right consistency. Season with salt and pepper.

FOR THE HERB AND GARLIC OIL

2 garlic gloves
250g spinach
50g parsley
50g basil leaves
25g tarragon
25g chives
300g colza oil

Blitz all the ingredients in a blender and pour into a plastic container. Cook in the microwave for 1 minute. Pass through a sieve, discarding the sediment. Allow to cool.

TO PLATE

Place 6 tablespoons of the marinera sauce on the plate, and arrange 10 mussels, cooked in the pan, on top. Trickle the herb and garlic oil around.

Willem Hiele.

WILLEM HIELE RESTAURANT, OUDENBURG (BE)

Willem Hiele grew up in a family of fisherman, and first opened his eponymous restaurant in his parents' old cottage near Ostend in 2015. Nicknamed the Flemish Viking, Hiele finds inspiration in the rich bounty of the North Sea and his large herb garden. He quickly won plaudits for his cuisine, earning him a Michelin star in 2021. He has since moved his restaurant into a brutalist building by Jacques Moeschal, in a nearby nature reserve.

—— 'I generally don't like making dishes over and over again, but you can consider this bisque as my signature dish,' explains Belgian chef Willem Hiele. 'When I was a child, my parents used to take me to visit my granduncle, Ferdinand Hiele. These visits always brought a smile to my face. Ferdinand had spent 39 years as a skipper in Icelandic waters. As soon as we drove up to his house and I opened the car door, I could smell the salt on the fishing nets that were hanging between the poplars to dry in the wind. Inside, my uncle 'Ferna' would be, enjoying a 'poester', alternating a sip of coffee with a sip of Bressac brandy. My grandmother, Mé, would be sitting across from him peeling freshly cooked shrimps to make soup from the heads and the shells. Even the neighbours could smell the captivating aroma.'

Hand-peeled shrimps are known as the caviar of the North Sea, but Hiele prefers to sing the praises of the 'little kellen', a small pool of seawater left behind on the beach when the tide goes out. The chef, who fell into cooking after being sent to work in a local bakery as a punishment for a misdemeanour, is known for coaxing out the best of the flavours of local ingredients from his terroir, using simple cooking techniques, such as his 'seafire' method, which allows fresh fish to be grilled, smoked and steamed at the same time.

'The story of this house is inextricably bound up with shrimps,' continues Hiele. 'Over the years, I have repeatedly refined the soup, which was always simmering on the hob. Shrimp soup is usually made with the remains of the heads and shells of cooked peeled shrimp. But I decided to use raw shrimp, because when you work with cooked shrimp, you lose a third of its flavour. My shrimp bisque takes me back to my childhood, filling me with nostalgia, and I am very keen to share that feeling with my guests. If only Mé was here to witness the reduction in decibels in her grandson's restaurant when we serve her wonderful soup.'

WILLEM HIELE - RESTAURANT WILLEM HIELE

Shrimp bisque.

SERVES 4

FOR THE BISQUE

3kg tiny raw shrimps
1 head of garlic, cut in half, crushed and finely chopped
3 chilies, finely chopped
200g tomato purée
olive oil, to taste

Heat the oil in a wide, deep pan. Fry the raw shrimps with the finely chopped garlic and chilies for about 5 minutes until you smell the captivating aroma of grilled shrimp. Add the tomato purée and stir well. Allow the tomato purée to caramelize with the rest. Add enough water to cover. Simmer very gently for 25 minutes. Remove from the heat and leave to cool for 1½–2 hours. Pour through a sieve and then boil down the liquid until it tastes right. Put in the refrigerator.
Repeat this process the next day and the day after. Combine all three bisques and bring them to the boil again.

FOR THE COFFEE CREAM

200ml whipped cream
2 tbsp cold coffee
Salt and pepper, to taste

Whip the cream with salt and pepper. Towards the end add 2 tablespoons of cold coffee.

TO SERVE

Serve the bisque in pretty porcelain teacups and garnish with the coffee cream. Serve with sourdough bread, hand-peeled shrimp and stockfish butter.

Dan Hunter.

BRAE, MELBOURNE (AU)

Australian chef Dan Hunter started his career as a dishwasher, later landing a job at Mugaritz in Spain. He opened Brae in Birregurra, Victoria, in 2013 and in 2017 it was selected as one of the World's 50 Best Restaurants.

— 'I'm not sure I want to say that we have a signature dish at Brae, but if I had to choose it's probably the parsnip and apple, currently served as the final dish on most menus,' says Hunter, who credits his transformation from pot scrubber to award-winning chef to his stint working under Philippe Mouchel and the late Jeremy Strode at the Melbourne restaurant Langton's.

'I don't really know how this dish is still around, but some guests come to the restaurant just to eat it, and as every plate is placed before them, they ask: "Is this the parsnip?" And sometimes, when the dish is brought to the table after they've spent a couple of hours in the dining room, they say: "Finally... I only came here for this."'

Hunter first started experimenting with the root vegetable before he opened Brae, frying a parsnip skin and then loading it with blueberries, fennel and crème fraiche. 'When I began developing the menu for Brae, I decided I wanted to turn the parsnip upside down as a gesture to myself and our team that we were about to turn everything on its head,' explains Hunter. 'I could see this beautiful immaculate golden shape in my head, and because it was so vivid in my mind I didn't really give it any proper development time.'

At Brae's soft opening, the dish was meant to be the last dessert, but Hunter and his team decided it was too terrible to serve: 'I left that night knowing that the menu was a dish short. I went home and drew diagram after diagram of plates, thinking about various nuances of the same ingredients that make that dish. I pretty much stayed up all night.' The next day Hunter made a fresh mousse with the apple and parsnip purée, adding lots of freeze-dried apple, 'which really gave it the lift that was previously missing' and served it with chamomile caramel. 'The presentation seemed so obvious at that moment that I was a little pissed off with myself for not getting there sooner.'

Over time the dish has evolved into a cannoli-shaped dessert. But 'unfortunately we can never reduce the time it takes to clean and trim the parsnips at this stage; it's one of the simplest yet tedious two-ingredient dishes on our menu.'

DAN HUNTER - BRAE

Parsnip and apple.

SERVES 4

FOR THE PARSNIPS

4 large parsnips

Place the parsnips in a baking tray, place a lid on top and steam for around 1 hour. Remove the lid and dry excess moisture from the parsnips by baking them at 100 °C (480 °F) for a further 45 minutes. Once cool, cut through the skin on one side, remove the core and all the flesh, ensuring that the skin remains intact and in one piece. Carefully scrape any remains of the flesh from the skin, slice the skins lengthways so that there are two equal halves and leave them to dry a little. Once semi-dried, fry the skins at 150 °C (300 °F), almost blanching them a little at a time. Due to the sugar in the parsnip, too much continuous time in the hot oil will burn the skin. Once a golden 'pastry' colour is achieved and while the skin is still hot, shape it into the desired concaved or cylinder shape and place to cool on absorbent paper. The finished crisp skin should be returned to its original shape, so that it appears as though it has been hollowed out, or if you prefer, to resemble the shape of cannoli. Leave in a dehydrator until needed.

FOR THE APPLE AND PARSNIP MOUSSE

2 egg yolks
36g caster sugar
24g water
½ sheet (1g) gold-leaf gelatine
20g apple pure
12.5g parsnip pure
4g freeze-dried apple powder
75g semi-whipped cream
salt to taste

In an electric beater, whisk the cream so that it forms soft peaks and reserve in a cool place.
Soak the gelatine in cold water and, once hydrated, remove it, squeezing out the excess moisture. Set aside.
Combine the sugar and water in a pan and place on a medium heat. While the sugar is warming, place the egg yolks in an electric beater and begin to beat on a medium speed. Heat the sugar to 120 °C (248 °F), turn off the heat and add the gelatine to the sugar. Once the gelatine has dissolved, lower the speed slightly on the egg yolk, and drizzle the sugar between the beater and the side of the bowl, taking care not to hit the beater. Once all the sugar is incorporated, place the beater on maximum speed and beat the eggs until they are shiny, have increased 6–8 times in volume, and are almost white.
Fold in the apple and parsnip purées, the freeze-dried apple powder and a little of the cream. When combined well, fold in the rest of the cream until the mixture is homogenous.
Place the mixture into a piping bag and reserve refrigerated until needed.

FOR THE APPLE AND
CAMOMILE INFUSION

4 Granny Smith apples
450g filtered water
12g camomile flowers
50g caster sugar

Bring the water to the boil and pour it over the camomile flowers. Cover immediately and leave to infuse for 6 minutes. Once infused, discard the camomile flowers and combine the infusion with the sugar and peeled apples.
Place the ingredients into a vacuum bag and seal on maximum pressure. Cook at 82 °C (180 °F) for 1.5 hours. Strain and discard the apples and chill immediately. Store covered and refrigerated until required.

FOR THE APPLE CARAMEL

450g apple/camomile infusion
50g caster sugar

Caramelise the sugar in a wide-based pan until it is a deep, dark golden colour. Deglaze with the apple infusion and allow to reduce to a thick caramel. Store covered at room temperature.

FOR THE FREEZE-DRIED APPLE

6 freeze-dried apple quarters
(3 cut into 12 pieces and
2 quarters left whole for grating)

TO PLATE

In the centre of a flat plate, pipe some of the mousse (around 10 cm) and drizzle the caramel over and around the mousse. Place 3 pieces of freeze-dried apple on and around the mousse, and then lay a piece of parsnip over the top so that the other ingredients are hidden underneath. Grate one half of a piece of freeze-dried apple over the parsnip and serve.

Supaksorn 'Ice' Jongsiri.

SORN, BANGKOK (TH)

Born in Bangkok and raised in Nakhon Si Thammarat, Supaksorn 'Ice' Jongsiri learned all about delicious Southern Thai cuisine from his grandmother, the founder of the Baan Ice restaurant where Jongsiri started his career after a stint in the US (where he worked as a Thai chef to fund his studies). Success was swift, and soon opened seven more Baan Ice eateries, as well as Sorn in Bangkok in 2018, which now boasts two Michelin stars.

—— Like all his chefs, self-trained wunderkind Supaksorn 'Ice' Jongsiri studied cooking with his grandmother. It's the best way to preserve the traditions of Southern Thailand, which is at the core of his culinary approach. 'My philosophy is to cook authentic Thai, using only Thai ingredients – if something has no Thai name, such as a carrot, I won't use it,' he says. 'It's not arrogance but to prove that Thai food as it is can be world-stage fine dining.'

After his university studies, the chef took over his grandmother's restaurant to great acclaim and decided to quit his desk job. 'I have much more to learn, but my love for food is real,' he says. 'My favourite ingredients are all things coconut – coconut water/ fresh coconut milk, shrimp paste (Kapi in Thai) and shellfish.' But also key to his cooking is an element which is often lacking today, namely time. 'We use the old styles of cooking, which takes more time and energy, but it means that anyone who cooks with me, cooks from the heart,' he explains. 'It's like grandmothers anywhere in the world; they cook from the morning and then the food magically appears for dinner. They take the time to cook for their family... it is love, the most powerful thing in the world. I will always cook with love, and if one day, I no longer cook with love, I will stop.'

When asked to select his signature dish, Jongsiri first thought about steamed crab knuckle, coated in yellow chilli paste and crab roe, but then settled on this colourful salad, featuring lotus stems, crispy turmeric rice, water mimosa and green mango. The story goes that a general in the military back in the day wanted to improve his diet as he wasn't eating enough vegetables. This was the origin of the creation of this dish, which contains over 10 herbs/spices locally grown in the south.' It's the essence of Jongsiri's cooking, which is 'comforting, simple and rustic with no shortcuts'.

SUPAKSORN 'ICE' JONGSIRI - SORN

'The sea holds the forest'.

SERVES 3 - 4

FOR THE CRISPY RICE COOKED
WITH TURMERIC WATER

Hom Mali rice (jasmine rice)
fresh, cold water
galangal
rice bran oil

Soak the jasmine rice in fresh water, then rinse twice to clean the rice. Drain and air-dry for 30 minutes.
Cook the rice in water seasoned with turmeric, and when the rice is cooked, spread it out thinly in a bamboo basket and leave to dry in the sun for 3 days. Once the rice is completely dry, fry in rice bran oil over a low heat until crispy.

FOR THE BOODOO SAUCE

galangal
lemongrass
shallots
garlic
young ginger in palm sugar
boodoo paste
grilled fish meat
palm sugar
shrimp paste
kaffir-lime leaves

Pound the galangal, lemongrass, shallots, garlic, and young ginger in a mortar until they are well combined.
In a pan, bring the boodoo paste, grilled fish meat, palm sugar, shrimp paste and pounded herbs to a boil, then reduce heat and simmer for 5 minutes.
Add the kaffir-lime leaves and simmer for another minute, then strain the sauce through a fine sieve and allow to cool.

FOR THE YUM RICE

crispy rice (see above)
cucumber, peeled, seeded and diced
lotus stem, thinly sliced
yard long beans, thinly sliced
pomelo and/or santol (peeled and seeded), flesh only
lemongrass, thinly sliced
water mimosa, thinly sliced
green mango, thinly sliced
kaffir lime leaves, thinly sliced
padaek sprouts
dried shrimp, toasted and ground
dried chili, toasted and ground
coconut, toasted and ground
lime

Mix all the ingredients.

SIGNATURE DISHES — 133

Hiroyasu Kawate.

FLORILÈGE, TOKYO (JP)

Born and raised in Tokyo, Hiroyasu Kawate is the chef-owner of Florilège, a French restaurant in Tokyo's Jingumae district. A champion of regional and urban sustainability, he delights in finding new value in familiar vegetables.

—— Hiroyasu Kawate is a man on a mission, advocating an urban version of sustainability through his fine dining. 'We have been trying to promote sustainable development and environment for years,' explains the Michelin-starred chef. 'We cherish our ingredients and we strive to minimise food waste, while delivering delicious dishes.'

His signature dish — beef carpaccio, or sustainability beef - encapsulates his thoughtful approach to the environment. It is is served with an accompanying note that highlights the issue of food waste, stating that 'Today in Japan, there are about 17 million tonnes of food waste per year, of which about 5-8 million tonnes are estimated to be expired edible foods. This amount is comparable to the total food consumption of the three countries of Namibia, Liberia and Congo. It is also about twice the amount of food aid worldwide.' It's a sobering snippet of information to receive at a fine-dining restaurant, but Kawate believes we can transmit bits of awareness through food and is convinced 'we can change the Earth by the way we eat and drink.'

The dish features Wagyu beef — marbled meat known for its tenderness and flavour. 'The reality is that little people know that Wagyu cows are raised in an artificial, non-sustainable environment, and that the mothers are traditionally discarded because it's thought that their meat is tough and tasteless,' explains the chef. 'So, I decided to design a sustainable dish using this normally discarded, fattened cow by letting it lead a healthy and happy life, free of artificial additives, and use them after their natural death for a dish honouring their subtle yet sophisticated taste. At the restaurant we serve the meat with a consommé sauce made from vegetable scraps.'

While not busy repurposing food scraps into culinary gems, Kawate runs cooking classes for non-professionals, teaching them how to make the best of seasonal fare and reduce food waste. 'My role as a chef is adding value to common ingredients; my favourites are potato, carrot and onion. Helped by the four Japanese seasons, I present them to the guests with the charm of my country through my personal filter.'

HIROYASU KAWATE - FLORILÈGE

Sustainability beef.

SERVES 4

FOR THE BEEF CARPACCIO

200g beef loin
salt, as needed
trehalose, as needed

Slice the beef loin into 5mm-thick slices and pound thinly with a meat hammer. Sprinkle the beef with salt and trehalose (yeast sugar), place on a wire rack, and allow the salt and trehalose to dry in. Set aside in a cool place for 6 hours.

FOR THE POTATO ESPUMA

250g potatoes, peeled
125g milk
125g double cream
3g salt
straw

Put the peeled potatoes and water in a pan and simmer until cooked. Mix the cooked potatoes with a hand blender and strain. Put in a cooking tray and smoke with straw. Put in an espuma syphon, keep it in hot water and set aside.

FOR THE CONSOMMÉ

1L fond de veau, *warmed*
300g minced beef shank
100g egg white
100g onion
50g celery
50g carrot
100g beetroot
50g tomato
1 sprig of tarragon
1 sprig of thyme

Heat the *fond de veau* to 40 °C (104 °F). Set aside.
Put the ground beef shank, vegetable scraps and herbs in another saucepan and mix well with your hands. Little by little, add the egg white to the mixture of meat and vegetables, mixing well each time.
Gradually add the warm *fond de veau*, then heat until 70 °C (158 °F), blending thoroughly. Stop mixing and bring almost to the boil. Simmer for 1 hour. Strain through a paper towel to remove all solid ingredients.

FOR THE PARSLEY OIL

100g parsley
150g sunflower oil

Blend the parsley and sunflower oil. Strain through a paper towel.

TO PLATE

Syphon the potato espuma onto the plate and arrange the beef carpaccio on top of it. Decorate with herbs and parsley oil and pour round the consommé.

SIGNATURE DISHES — 137

Santiago Lastra.

KOL, LONDON (UK)

Born in Mexico City, Santiago Lastra began working in professional kitchens at the age of 15, then spent four years travelling the world and training at institutions including San Sebastian's Mugaritz. As René Redzepi's right-hand man, he helped launch Noma Mexico pop-up restaurant in 2017. The chef came up with the idea for Kol on a beach in Tulum, and in 2020 he opened the restaurant in London's foodie district of Marylebone.

× **What does your signature dish tell us about?**

SANTIAGO LASTRA: *It's a marriage between Mexico and England, and a way to transport the guests to two of my favourite experiences ever: eating lobster tacos in Baja California on the beach, and freshly caught langoustine by the sea in Scotland. These places also inspired me to pick berries on the beach - from sea bucktorn bushes - and squeeze them on my tacos.*

× **How would you describe your cooking and your philosophy?**

SANTIAGO LASTRA: *Mexican soul, British ingredients. We take inspiration from Mexican flavours and we apply that to British seasonal ingredients to bring together the best of both cultures.*

I am from Mexico but I've been living outside my country for 14 years, so my approach to cooking was born out of the need to eat and cook Mexican food outside my country. Through my experience, I realised that Mexican food is more related to a culture than to specific ingredients. So, it is my intention to focus on the Mexican flavour experience and translate it using local seasonal ingredients.

× **What is the story behind your signature dish?**

SANTIAGO LASTRA: *It was a quest to find a dish that could represent our concept: using British ingredients reflecting Mexican tastes, and be subtle, elegant and elevated, yet pretty approachable. I knew the dish had to be a taco.*

I thought about my favourite ingredients and I put them together in a dish that is dedicated to my two sources of inspiration: Mexico and my roots, and the UK and its wonderful ingredients.

× **How and when did you become passionate about food?**

SANTIAGO LASTRA: *I was 15. My family didn't cook. I went to the supermarket and bought a packet of Ritz crackers and on the back was a recipe for a crab dip. I decided to buy all the ingredients and cook them at home. My family liked it, so I went back to the supermarket to get some recipe booklets. I cooked everything I could ... Then I started working in an Italian restaurant to see if cooking was what I wanted to pursue as a profession.*

When my dad and both my grandparents passed away in the same month, I decided to stop school, spending all my time at the restaurant and brought home bread, wine and food for my mother and brother, and I remember watching them in the kitchen, smiling and happy. I thought that if I could make them happy at such a sad time by cooking, I could do the same for more people, and at that moment I decided to dedicate my life to food, to learn and travel and try to become the best version of myself.

× **Which cuisines influenced your cooking?**

SANTIAGO LASTRA: *Mexican of course, because it's a constant, endless source of inspiration. I have had the opportunity to travel around Mexico and visit indigenous communities; spending time with them and learning from them. Its essence is totally priceless.*

My father and his family were from Spain, and I started cooking more professionally when I moved there when I was 18. Spanish cuisine is the food of my childhood and a key to the way I cook today.

And last but not least, Nordic cuisine and its philosophy has also influenced me. I consider Copenhagen my second home; I lived in the city for over four years and most of my friends live there. I visit them when I have the chance. The way they put ingredients together and their respect for the craft of cooking and sourcing is a massive part of my personal ethos and philosophy.

× **What are the characteristics of the dishes you like to cook?**

SANTIAGO LASTRA: *I feel a responsibility to share stories and transport people to my country. I also look into clean flavours and seasonal ingredients to give the guests a sense of what is growing and happening around them in nature.*

I love using different types of chilis, not only to make my dishes spicy, but also to give them depth. I intend to make colourful, bright and refreshing food that makes people feel happy. My other favourite ingredients are roasted garlic and corn in all forms.

× **Which chefs do you admire?**

SANTIAGO LASTRA: *René Redzepi from Noma has given me the opportunity of a lifetime and has been a great support; I learned so much from him. Andoni Luis Aduriz and the team from Mugaritz, who taught me that there is nothing in this world that is impossible to cook when you have the right vision and perseverance. Pilar Idoate from Europa, who taught me to cook. All the indigenous cooks in Mexico who are a constant source of inspiration. There's a saying in the Totonacapan community of Veracruz: 'We are born, we live, we cook and we die in the kitchen', and that devotion to a lifetime of craft for generations is more than I could ever achieve. I will be forever thankful for the opportunity to learn from them.*

SANTIAGO LASTRA - KOL

Langoustine tacos.

SERVES 6

FOR THE CHIPOTLE CREAM

125g double cream
25g chipotle paste

To make the chipotle cream, simply mix the cream and chipotle paste together.

FOR THE SEA BUCKTHORN SYRUP

100g sea buckthorn juice, or tamarind paste
50g caster sugar
50g muscovado sugar

To make the sea buckthorn syrup, pour the juice and both sugars into a pan with 50ml water. Bring to a simmer, then reduce by three-quarters or until dark, thick and syrupy (be sure to keep an eye on it and stir regularly so it does not burn). Leave to cool then pass through a fine sieve into a squeezy bottle – you will probably have more than you need for this dish but it will last for months in the refrigerator.

FOR THE LANGOUSTINES

6 langoustines
rapeseed oil, for frying
1 garlic clove, finely sliced
1 pinch of langoustine powder or chicken bouillon powder (optional)
salt

Prepare the langoustines by placing them in the freezer for 20 minutes (this makes them easier to peel). If you are using live langoustines, humanely kill them and then separate the head from the tail. Carefully peel the tails, then set aside.
Place a frying pan over a medium heat and add the langoustine heads. Drizzle with a little rapeseed oil, then fry, turning occasionally, until cooked through but not dry. Lift them out of the pan and set aside.
In the same pan, add the sliced garlic and gently cook until lightly browned. Slice each langoustine tail into 3 pieces, then add these to the pan. Gently cook for around 30 seconds until just beginning to turn opaque, then pour in the chipotle cream and add a pinch of langoustine (or chicken bouillon) powder and a pinch of salt. Cook very briefly then remove from the heat.

TO FINISH AND PLATE

6 soft small tortillas
sea arrowgrass, torn into small pieces (or coriander or any other aromatic herb)
6 tbsp sauerkraut
samphire or sea purslane
1 tbsp sea buckthorn berries
sesame seeds, for sprinkling
chickweed
100ml sea buckthorn juice (or kumquat juice mixed with lime juice)

Place a clean dry frying pan over a high heat and allow to get very hot. Place the tortillas in the pan for a minute to heat through and soften, then remove.

In the same pan add the samphire and/or sea purslane and lightly fry in a splash of oil. Add the sea buckthorn berries and warm through, then set aside.

To build the tacos, place a spoonful of sauerkraut and a little sea arrowgrass into each taco. Place 3 pieces of langoustine on top, ensuring plenty of the chipotle cream is drizzled over. Add a small drizzle of reduced sea buckthorn juice (or tamarind), then sprinkle with sesame seeds. Finish with the fried samphire, sea purslane and buckthorn berries, followed by the chickweed.

Finally, to serve, fill a syringe with fresh sea buckthorn juice and inject it into the inside of the langoustine heads. Bring the tacos to the table with a langoustine head on the side – squeeze the heads over the tacos like a lime to add sourness and the richness of the langoustine head juices.

Corey Lee.

BENU, SAN FRANCISCO (US)

Born in 1977, Corey Lee is a Korean-American chef who worked at some of the most acclaimed restaurants in the world, including a tenure as a head chef at The French Laundry, where his work was recognized with a James Beard Award. His flagship restaurant, Benu, became the first in San Francisco to receive three Michelin stars 2014, making Lee the first Korean chef to garner this accolade.

—— Corey Lee's intriguing signature dish encapsulates his dual identity: 'The dish highlights that I'm bicultural; I was born in Korea and grew up in the US,' he says. 'I think it also reveals that I value tradition and I am also interested in how those traditions can evolve.'

Century eggs also known as preserved eggs, hundred-year eggs and thousand-year-old eggs, are an Asian delicacy featuring eggs that have been preserved for a long period of time in a curing mixture that traditionally includes clay, salt, wood ash and quicklime. As a result of the process, the eggs turn dark and gelatinous, and are packed full of flavour.

'Thousand-year-old eggs are bases and help awaken the palate,' says Lee. 'So, I always thought of using them for an opening to a menu. When I tried making one for the first time, I realised how complex and technical they are to make, so it really captured my interest and attention as a chef.' His version of the classic includes a quail egg preserved in a mix of p'u-erh tea, lye, salt and zinc for about a month and a half. The result is served with a bacon and cabbage potage, cabbage jus and ginger pickled in champagne vinegar.

The chef, who trained at fine-dining institutions such as Pied à Terre and The French Laundry with Thomas Keller, says he likes to 'explore how traditional and modern approaches to food can harmonise to yield something delicious, evocative and memorable.' He continues: 'As a younger chef, I valued originality above tradition and thought that it was okay to fail in the pursuit of something new. But now I feel that is a somewhat selfish and vain perspective. Now, both as a chef and as a diner, I'd rather have a traditional dish that's delicious and satisfying.'

Growing up in an immigrant family, Lee was always passionate about food: 'Trying to experience the flavours of our native culture while living abroad, we were constantly on the hunt for ingredients, grocery stores and restaurants so we could get a taste of good Korean food.' Among his favourite ingredients are the Asian staples: rice, soy sauce and chilli, but his inspiration also comes from Europe, and includes a great respect for the work of chefs such as Alain Passard, Michel Bras, René Redzepi and Albert Adrià.

COREY LEE - BENU

Thousand-year-old quail's eggs with potage and preserved ginger.

SERVES 50

FOR THE THOUSAND-YEAR-OLD
QUAIL'S EGGS

24 quail's eggs
330g water
1g pu-erh tea
14g sodium hydroxide (lye)
16g kosher salt
0.7g food-grade zinc

Bring half of the water to the boil in a saucepan, then remove from the boil and add the tea. Steep for 20 minutes, then add the salt, lye and zinc, and allow to dissolve. Add the remainder of the water. Pour the brine into a ceramic jar with a lid. The next day, submerge the eggs in the brine and keep the eggs in the brine for 12 days.

Remove the eggs from the brine and dip them in water to briefly rinse the shells. Air-dry the eggs for about 1 hour. Seal them in a plastic bag and store in a box that doesn't allow light to enter. Keep in a cool dry area for a minimum of 4 weeks.

Remove the eggs from storage and drop them into boiling water for 1 minute (don't allow the water to go off the boil). Plunge the eggs into an ice bath. Peel and cut in half.

FOR THE POTAGE

200g bacon, thinly sliced
700g green cabbage, thinly sliced
200g onion, thinly sliced
50g butter
1L chicken stock
7g salt
0.5g cayenne
100g hot cream

Sweat the bacon, cabbage and onion in the butter, making sure the vegetables have sweated through completely but not caramelised. Cover with chicken stock, then bring to a boil and reduce the mixture rapidly to 900g. Purée the mixture (including bacon) until smooth, adding the salt, cayenne and hot cream.

Pass the mixture through a fine sieve, then stir over an ice bath until completely chilled.

FOR THE GREEN CABBAGE JUICE

1 green cabbage, outer green layers removed (for the juice), the white inner layers finely diced and blanched in unsalted water for 1 minute
(According to the volume of juice:
1% salt
0.5% champagne vinegar
2% Ultratex starch)

Peel the outer part (green layers) of the cabbage, and blanch for 1 minute in boiling water. Plunge into an ice bath. Squeeze out excess water by hand and pat dry.
Next pass the cabbage through a juicer. Take all the pulp and run it through the juicer one more time, then pass the juice through a chinois. Add the seasonings, the Ultratex starch and finally the diced cabbage.

FOR THE PICKLED GINGER

1 medium-sized young ginger root, peeled
2 parts water
1 part champagne vinegar
1 part sugar

Slice the young ginger very thinly using a mandoline. Bring the water, vinegar and sugar to a boil, and pour the boiling pickling liquid over the ginger. Allow to cool to room temperature, and store in the refrigerator for at least 1 week. Strain and finely chop the ginger, reserving the juice.

TO PLATE

Place a dollop of chopped ginger in a small bowl, then add a large spoonful of heated potage on top. Cover the surface with the cabbage juice mixture. Season the egg half with the ginger pickling juice and salt, then place on top of the cabbage.

Ángel León.

APONIENTE, PUERTO DE SANTA MARÍA (ES)

Known in Spain as 'el Chef del Mar' for his visionary take on seafood dishes, Ángel León was born in 1977 in Jerez de la Frontera. Collaborating with universities and scientists, the chef is the first one to use plankton in a fine dining kitchen, and to create innovative saline cheese and cold cuts made out of seafood. Aponiente restaurant now has three Michelin Stars.

—— For his signature dish, Ángel León looked no further than his back garden, the Bahía de Cádiz Natural Park, an area of marshland inhabited by a myriad species of plants and animals. 'It's a creation which in a few bites you can capture the pure flavour of the environment that you see when you come to our restaurant, in an old tide mill in the middle of a nature reserve,' explains the revered Spanish chef. 'Our aim is for our guests to savour and appreciate the essence of the marshes.'

The marshes... and the sea, of course: 'This preparation shows a representation of plants and algae from our direct environment, it highlights other marine ingredients other than fish, which we commonly use at Aponiente. Taking advantage of the resources of our most immediate landscape, the marshes, we collect halophilic plants that grow in environments with salt water.'

The idea for this dish stems from the wish of León's team to recreate 'a 100% marine salad, with different textures and based on sea plants and algae.' The stunning result contains seaweed such as laurentia, aptenia or karkalla, depending on the season, as well as plankton oil, oyster dressing and oyster gelée. It joins creations such as sea bacon (sea bass prepared like bacon), sea ham (red tuna belly) and a 'crunchy' omelette with baby shrimp on an inventive tasting menu which León elaborates with his team of culinary scientists.

Over the last 11 years, León's research and development team has worked on over 30 projects with the aim of reducing fishing pressure and finding new sources of marine proteins, which includes work on phytoplankton and their natural pigments; fats of marine origin; marine honey and cereal, as well as techniques using microalgae and marine collagens.

León's Aponiente is not just a restaurant, but an ambitious project whose aim is to reactivate and recover the environment surrounding the restaurant by restoring the ecosystem and re-establishing the natural balance. León not only protects the fragile coastal wetlands, but its people too. Taking care of the natural capital of the marshes means bringing a source of income, wealth and employment for the area.

ÁNGEL LEÓN - APONIENTE

Sea salad.

SERVES 20

FOR THE OYSTER DRESSING

90g oysters
300g oyster water
5g lemon juice
180g sunflower oil
5g emulsifying paste
0.6g xanthan gum
salt

Crush the oyster in the Thermomix with the water, lemon juice and xanthan gum, emulsifying at medium speed with the sunflower oil. Next, add the emulsifier paste and blend to obtain a perfect cream. Strain through a Superbag and store ready for serving.

FOR THE PLANKTON OIL

350g sunflower oil
150g extra-virgin olive oil
20g plankton

Blend everything to achieve a smooth, homogenous consistency.

FOR THE HALOPHYTE AND SEAWEED SALAD (TYPES DEPENDING ON THE SEASON)

Laurentia
Aptenia *(in season)*
karkalla (beach banana)
Gigartina pistilata
Mertensia
sea purslane (halimione portulacoides)
sorrel
Vertebrata lanosa
glaucous phycoid

First hydrate the gelatine leaf in water and ice. Then strain the oyster water through a Superbag to remove the impurities. Divide the water equally between two saucepans. To one add the lemon juice and set aside at room temperature. Heat the other saucepan and bring the water up to 60 °C (140 °F), pass through the Superbag again and add the gelatine. Mix with the remaining oyster water and lemon juice. Place on a tray and leave to cool in the refrigerator. Before serving, break up with a fork.

FOR THE 'OYSTER WATER GELÉE'

100g oyster water
3g lemon juice
1 sheet of gelatine

TO PLATE

Arrange small fragments of each of the seaweeds and halophytes listed in the ingredients on the 'oyster water gelée'.

Richie Lin.

MUME, TAIPEI (TW)

Richie Lin was born in Hong Kong to Indonesian-Chinese parents, raised in Canada, and trained at Quay in Australia and Noma in Europe. After launching Nur in Hong Kong, he opened his first restaurant in Taiwan in 2014 with his Noma colleague Long Xiong and Quay pastry chef Ken Ken Ward. Today, the chef, named as one of the best in Asia, uses local produce in a Nordic style, with a zero-waste cooking practice and was rewarded with a Michelin star.

✕ What does your signature dish tell us about you?

RICHIE LIN: *For us, the design of the menu very much follows the seasons. We let nature guide us and we really focus on using as many Taiwanese ingredients as possible. Fruits and vegetables are of high quality in Taiwan, especially in the high mountains, that represent half of the island. Moreover, we have a wide variety of vegetables, and they are often picked and foraged by the indigenous people. My personal favourite is magao, a wild mountain pepper. It's aromatic with a strong citrus-ginger spiciness. It's only available in June and July, but we use it extensively in many different ways to make oils, pickles, desserts, cocktails... and in our MUME salad.*

✕ What is the story behind its creation?

RICHIE LIN: *I think our MUME salad represents a lot of what we do. It's composed of 20-30 different vegetables from Taiwan — some are fermented, others are raw, dried or fried. It's very much a spontaneous process, depending on what we receive from the farm. We also incorporate our culture using one of my favourite elements in Chinese cooking: fermented black beans. We dehydrate them to concentrate their flavour and use them like salt to season the salad.*

> FOR US, THE DESIGN OF THE MENU VERY MUCH FOLLOWS THE SEASONS, WE LET NATURE GUIDE US AND WE REALLY FOCUS ON USING AS MANY TAIWANESE INGREDIENTS AS POSSIBLE.

✕ **Where do you come from? What is your philosophy?**

RICHIE LIN: *I grew up in an Asian Family, and when I was 12 we moved to Canada. Living in a mixed background family in an immigrant country definitely opens a wide range of flavours.*

The older I get the more I appreciate the taste of umami, widely recognised as the fifth taste, and addictive to your taste buds. Some people think that Umami belongs to Asian cuisine, but it's universal. If you think cheese, ketchup, vegemite or anchovies taste great, in fact what you are choosing is the taste of umami. From a cook's perspective, its synergistic effect is really fascinating. The hearty, rich, round and altogether pleasant sensation is exactly what I intend to achieve in my cooking: it's always the core of my dish. I create it from natural ingredients, that I ferment or enhance by preserving, curing, dry-ageing or combining different umami-imparting substances together. With umami, 1+1 doesn't equal to 2; it is exponential you put the right ingredients together. It's fascinating.

✕ **How and when did you become passionate about food?**

RICHIE LIN: *To quote from our beloved Anthony Bourdain: 'Travel isn't always pretty. It isn't always comfortable. Sometimes it hurts, it even breaks your heart. But that's okay. The journey changes you; it should change you. It leaves marks on your memory, on your consciousness, on your heart, and on your body. You take something with you. Hopefully, you leave something good behind.' Travel is important, especially for chefs. It changes you in the most subtle way. I particularly like travelling alone.*

✕ **Was there one trip in particular that really inspired you?**

RICHIE LIN: *Last year I made my first ever trip to Mexico. I travelled there with no itinerary, no plans except a booked meal at Noma. Eventually it turned out to be one of my best travel experiences. During my stay in Mexico City, I spent two days at the National Museum of Anthropology, fascinated by how they documented in very precise detail how they cook and eat.*

I found that the fruit and vegetables in Mexico have a lot of similarities to those in Taiwan. It inspired me to try using their cooking techniques. When I got back, I did some research on nixtamalisation (a traditional maize preparation process in which dried kernels are cooked and steeped in an alkaline solution), using something that belongs to Taiwan. I'm trying different grains, such as rice, wheat and legumes.

✕ **Did this research evolve into a specific dish?**

RICHIE LIN: *It was a long process and I thought I would never be able to make a nice tortilla. After countless failures we came across a very interesting grain, a type of red quinoa that is widely consumed by the indigenous peoples of Taiwan. After the nixtamalisation of the grain we made a masa [maize dough] and hand-pressed it to make it nice and thin. I really liked the toasted flavour after the quinoa was fried so we then decided to make it a tostada instead of a tortilla. The quinoa tostada has been on our menu ever since, together with a a Wagyu tartare that incorporates Taiwanese traditional condiments. This dish is purely inspired by my experience in Mexico, yet it's so close to home, here in Taiwan.*

MUME salad.

The MUME salad is composed of 20–30 different seasonal vegetables from Taiwan: some fermented, some raw, some dried or fried … everything according to what we have received from the farm that day. We season the salad using one of my favourite ingredients in Chinese cooking – fermented black beans, which we have dehydrated to concentrate the flavour, using it just like salt.

So, there is no 'recipe' as such. Rather, the preparation of the salad is entirely spontaneous, with the cooking method of each ingredient decided after we have received the produce, because sometimes we don't know what we are getting.

50 CHEFS SHARE THEIR SECRET RECIPES

Virgilio Martínez.

CENTRAL, LIMA (PE)

Born in Lima in 1977, Virgilio Martínez worked in New York, Bogota and Madrid before opening Central in 2008. It was named Best Restaurant in Latin America in 2014, and number 2 of The World's 50 Best List in 2022. Today, Virgilio Martínez and his wife Pia León celebrate the unique landscapes, history and traditions of Peru, applying modern cooking techniques to indigenous Peruvian ingredients such as high-altitude potatoes and wild varieties of kiwicha and quinoa.

× **What does your signature dish tell us about you?**

VIRGILIO MARTÍNEZ VÉLIZ: *The dish is a representation of my emotions when I get to explore a region I didn't know much about, such as the Amazonian jungle. I truly enjoy this discovery, not only because I get to know a new place, but also because I get to discover new things, learning from the native Amazonian communities around.*

× **What is the story behind its creation?**

VIRGILIO MARTÍNEZ VÉLIZ: *The goal of the dish is to recreate an ecosystem and integrate it into our environment here in the restaurant. For this creation in particular, the purpose is to represent the lower jungle. We use ingredients that can be found in the area such as yuca (also known as cassava), Amazonian fish, and tucupi, which is made of a fermentation technique unique in the area. The locals take the yuca, and ferment it to achieve an explosion of umami flavour, similar to black garlic. We create a sauce using this ingredient, which is emulsified with the fish's bone marrow — found in the head, bones and cheeks of the fish — for a deeper and richer flavour. Finally, we season it with salt and spices found in the jungle.*

X **Where do you come from and what is your philosophy?**

VIRGILIO MARTÍNEZ VÉLIZ: *I'm Peruvian. I was born and raised in Lima, but draw my inspiration from the whole country of Peru: the territory, the people, the ingredients, the culture – all of these inspire me. I take what I learn from my travels and integrate it into our cuisine. The idea is also to introduce our local cuisine to different parts of the world, and create a sort of global manifestation of what we do here.*

X **How would you describe your cooking?**

VIRGILIO MARTÍNEZ VÉLIZ: *We want to immerse our guests in Peru and its biodiversity by describing and analysing what goes on there. To do so, we dive deep into nature, doing our best to gain a better and deeper understanding of the environment. We then express what we learned in the best way we can, through our dishes. Our research involves different perspectives, not only from a gastronomic point of view, but also from different fields and disciplines, in order to understand and look better into the roots of where our food comes from.*

We tell the story of our country's natural biodiversity, and present the different dishes as close to what you can expect when you go there. We want to provide an educational experience, and invoke a sense of place, through the joy, happiness and sensibility you can get from tasting the food here.

X **How and when did you become passionate about food?**

VIRGILIO MARTÍNEZ VÉLIZ: *In Peruvian culture, food is incredibly important and a way of bonding with your family. My passion began when I was very young: I still remember the first time I sat at the dinner table with my family, sharing many memories with them over a meal.*

X **Which cuisines influenced your cooking?**

VIRGILIO MARTÍNEZ VÉLIZ: *I began my career cooking classic French cuisine. I then moved to different parts of the world, such as Spain Southeast Asia and Japan.*

I was inspired by these travels of course. However, my first love remains local Peruvian cuisine. Since I came back to Peru, 15 years ago, I have had the wonderful opportunity to travel to different places in the country, learning what it had to offer. Over the years, I have had the chance to work with different ingredients, mostly from the Amazon and the Andes.

IN PERUVIAN CULTURE, FOOD IS INCREDIBLY IMPORTANT, AND A WAY OF BONDING WITH YOUR FAMILY. I STILL REMEMBER THE FIRST TIME I SAT AT THE DINNER TABLE WITH MY FAMILY, SHARING MANY MEMORIES WITH THEM OVER A MEAL.

X **What are the characteristics of the dishes you like to cook?**

VIRGILIO MARTÍNEZ VÉLIZ: *Balance is the recurring theme of all the dishes we create at the restaurant. We are always searching for harmony between the ingredients, colours, tastes, stories, ideas and authenticity. These elements are all crucial because they create the soul and essence of every plate. We get to work with so many wonderful ingredients that we have here, but I am partial to native potatoes, scallops and cauliflower. Apart from the consistency of all the dishes we put out, our intention is to tell a story and create dishes with character.*

X **What is your best quality as a chef?**

VIRGILIO MARTÍNEZ VÉLIZ: *I am a good student, always eager to learn something new. Even at 44 years old, there is still so much I can learn from everyone. I am always conversing with people, listening to them and really taking in what they have to share.*

X **What is your main concern: originality or respect for tradition?**

VIRGILIO MARTÍNEZ VÉLIZ: *I don't believe we have to choose between one or the other because both of them play a role in today's gastronomy. Though we can be innovative, progressive and original, I believe that we also need to respect and preserve the traditions that came before us.*

SIGNATURE DISHES —— 161

VIRGILIO MARTÍNEZ VÉLIZ - CENTRAL

Amazonian fish and tucupi.

SERVES 10

FOR THE MISHKINA AND
TUCUPI CRACKER

40g mishkina (mix of Amazonian herbs and spices)
200g tucupi
1kg fermented cassava (made of 350g raw peeled cassava, 650ml water and 20g salt)
300g tapioca
1.5L fermented cassava juice

For the fermented cassava juice, put 350g raw peeled cassava, 650ml water and 20g salt into a sealed container or a vacuum bag for at least 15 days. Put the mishkina, the water, 800g of the cassava ferment, the cassava juice (made using a juice extractor) and 250g tapioca into a saucepan, and heat until homogeneous. When the tapioca is fully activated and starts to thicken the mix, spread the mix into Silpats.
Mix the rest of the ingredients in another saucepan and cook in same way. Then add thin strips of the black mixture on top of the yellow one while still hot.
Dehydrate the mixture on the Silpats until completely dry. Let them rest uncovered in the fridge for at least 24 hours and the fry the sheets of mishkina and tucupi at 180 °C (355 °F). Reserve in a dry, warm place.

FOR THE PAICHE DEMI

1kg onions
750g carrots
500g celery
200g garlic
1L red wine
bones of a whole paiche (pirarucu)

Burn the bones of the paiche in the oven until golden brown. Deglaze the tray with the wine.
Chop the vegetables into big chunks and roast in the oven. Combine the vegetables with the bones, cover with water, then bring to a gentle simmer. After 2 hours, strain the bones and vegetables. At this point, reserve 500ml of liquid for the tucupi air.
Reduce the remainder gently until thick and silky.

FOR THE TUCUPI AIR

600ml Amazonian nuts milk
400g tucupi
4 egg whites

Mix all the ingredients in a pan and then set over the heat. Gently bring the mixture up to 65 °C (150 °F) so the egg whites can do their work.
Once it hits the needed temperature, using a hand blender, whisk the mixture and use the air that is going to build on top of the liquid for plating.

FOR THE PAICHE HEAD

After soaking the paiche head in iced water for 12–24 hours, pat it dry and put under the grill on a medium to low heat, making sure you get the middle part cooked through.

Since the different parts of the head have different cooking times, remove and reserve the cheeks as soon as they are done and then put the rest of head back under the grill.

After about 2–3 hours of cooking, extract the bone marrow from the forehead of the fish and reserve.

FOR THE PAICHE SAUCE

200ml paiche demi
50g paiche bone marrow
1 bitter orange, zest only

Heat the paiche demi in a saucepan, and then, off the heat, add the cold bone marrow to emulsify the sauce.

Finish the sauce with fresh zest from a whole bitter orange.

TO PLATE

Warm the paiche cheeks in the sauce at a low temperature, making sure the sauce doesn´t separate. Place the cheeks along with a good spoonful of the sauce in the bottom of each dish. Add crushed pieces of the mishkina and tucupi cracker. Top with tucupi air and garnish with flowers.

Dabiz Muñoz.

DIVERXO, MADRID (ES)

Born in Madrid in 1980, Dabiz Muñoz worked at Nobu and Hakkasan in London before heading home to open Diverxo in 2007. Known for his artistic avant-garde cuisine, mixed with Asian influences, the chef won his third Michelin star in 2013, and his restaurant was ranked number 4 on The World's 50 Best List 2022.

—— 'My philosophy is creativity, avant-garde, surprise, risk,' says David Muñoz, the wildly inventive Spanish chef whose personal appearance, complete with mohawk and countless ear piercings, reinforces his adventurous reputation. Using seasonal products from small producers, the Madrilenian chef creates dishes full of flavour and drama, such as The Ages of Hake, of which he says: 'It's a dish that brings together everything I want Diverxo to be in terms of creativity, flavour and use of ingredients.'

With this dish Muñoz aims to use the different parts of the fish to maximum effect: using the hake tripe, neck and head to make a yellow pil-pil sauce; curing its roe; and turning its offcuts into a *leche de tigre* marinade and its cheeks into a sauce and garnishes. The dish's spotless composition is also the perfect representation of Muñoz's obsession for perfection.

'Diverxo's current menu is like Black Mirror: self-conclusive stories that share the same DNA, yet are independent chapters of each other; each dish at Diverxo could exist on its own and anywhere on the menu,' explains the chef, who fell in love with cooking after repeated childhood visits to Restaurante Viridiana, one of Madrid's leading fine-dining institutions. There he fell under the spell of Abraham García's cuisine, which reflects the chef's varied interests, from literature to photography, as well as his passion for fresh, local ingredients.

Talking about ingredients, Muñoz's favourites are chillies, to maximise the flavours; citrus, to lighten the dish (Diverxo uses up to 15 different kinds of citrus fruits on a menu on any given day: lime, lemon, kaffir lime, mandarin or calamansi among them); and Jamón ibérico, dubbed the perfect product, versatile and full of flavour.

Other formative experiences of his include travelling around the world, and stints at Mugaritz and Hakkasan in London, where he realised his forte was to cook freely, combining techniques and approaches from various countries. No wonder Diverxo has been described as a slightly psychedelic 'journey around the world', where guests are never quite sure where they stand. Its 12-course tasting menu that presents dishes arranged like artworks on the blank canvas of a plate, has helped turn the Spanish capital into a top dining destination.

DABIZ MUÑOZ - DIVERXO

The Ages of Hake.

SERVES 4

FOR THE YELLOW PIL-PIL

2 heads of garlic
200g shallot
200g leek
2kg hake neck and head
200kg cod tripe
200ml olive oil
200ml garlic oil*
500g fresh yellow aji *(horse mackerel)*
20g fish sauce
10g purple shiso *(beefsteak plant)*

Put the cod tripe in a pot with water and cook for at least 1 hour. Drain and put the cod stock and the tripe to one side separately.
Clean the yellow *aji*. Remove the seeds and the veins – you will be left with roughly 200g. Blanch, plunge in water and ice to chill and then liquidise in a food processor with the cod tripe. Put to one side.
Put 200ml of olive oil and 50ml of garlic oil into a large pot. Add the heads of garlic and brown. Add the leek and the shallot until sautéed. Add the hake neck and head with the skin down and lower the heat. Add the yellow aji and tripe mixture. Leave to cook on a low heat for 40 minutes.
Once cooked, strain through a sieve, pressing down hard to get all the stock out. Emulsify in the blender, trickling in the remaining garlic oil. Add the fish sauce and chopped purple *shiso*.

*GARLIC OIL

1kg heads of garlic
2.5L olive oil

Cut the heads of garlic in half and put into a pot. Cover with the olive oil and cook on a low heat for 3 hours.

FOR THE CURED HAKE ROE

1kg plump hake roe
2kg coarse salt
100g lyophilised (freeze-dried) beetroot
40g chipotle chilli powder
water

Cover the hake roe with the salt for 5 hours. Remove the roe and wash with water. Air in a cold room for 7 days. Smoke for 4 minutes, then air for another 2 days.
Mix the beetroot and chipotle with the water. Coat the roe with the mixture and air for 2 more days.

FOR THE HAKE FAT POWDER

4 hake heads
2kg hake bones
2L olive oil
200g garlic
50g parsley
100ml garlic oil
800g maltodextrin

Clean the hake heads, Put in water and ice and bleed for 24 hours. Next, put the hake heads in vacuum bags, cover with olive oil and seal. Place in the 100% steam oven to cook at 80 °C (176 °F) for 6 hours. Strain and decant, putting the fat to one side. Bleed the bones for 24 hours.
Mash the garlic, parsley and garlic oil together. Marinate the bones with the mash for 4 hours. Brown the bones with the fat from the hake heads. Drain and add the maltodextrin.

FOR THE LECHE DE TIGRE
(TIGER'S MILK)

BASE

1L lime juice
1L white fish stock
45g garlic, clove germs removed
15g coriander stalks
1 Thai chilli pepper
200g fish (hake) offcuts

Liquidise all the ingredients in a blender and sieve.

FINAL TOUCH

400g fresh yellow aji (200g when deseeded and blanched once)
320g leche de tigre base
25g garlic
30g ginger

Add the remaining ingredients to the base and liquidise until well blended.

FOR THE CHEEK SAUCE

300g garlic à la brunoise (cut into 3mm cubes)
500g carrots à la brunoise
15 vine tomatoes
2 white onions, julienned
150g ginger à la brunoise
750ml Oloroso sherry wine
6g La Vera paprika
10g chipotle chilli paste
500g hake cheeks
250g buffalo milk butter
500g striped Venus clams
2kg red scorpion fish or rock fish
1L olive oil

Put the red scorpion fish in water and ice with 30% salt for 12 hours.
Oven-roast the vine tomatoes at 180 °C (350 °F) for 25 minutes.
Put the olive oil in a wide, deep pan, add the red scorpion fish and fry until golden. Add the garlic, ginger and clams. When the clams open, add the carrot and sauté.
Toast the paprika and chipotle on one side of the pan. Add the onion, the oven-roasted tomatoes and the Oloroso sherry wine, then cover and cook for at least 45–50 minutes. Turn off the heat and leave to rest for 8 hours. Strain. Add the cheeks and 250g of buffalo milk butter and leave to cook for 45 minutes. Strain and emulsify in a blender.

FOR THE BUTTER FOAM

1kg butter
15g soy lecithin
20g Sucro Emul (sugar emulsion)

Melt the butter at 75–80 °C (165–175 °F) degrees, add the lecithin and Sucro Emul, then liquidise in a blender until the butter becomes foamy.

FOR THE BLACK GARLIC MAYONNAISE

125g sunflower oil
250g olive oil
50g pasteurised egg white
30g pasteurised egg yolk
5g salt
10g black garlic cloves

Liquidise the egg yolk and egg white together with the salt and garlic in a blender or food processor. When the mixture is well liquidised and smooth, add the oils gradually to create the mayonnaise.

FOR THE SMOKED POTATO POWDER

800g Monalisa potatoes
200g Agria potatoes
50g squid ink
vine shoots, for smoking

Peel the Agria potatoes and bake the skins in the oven at 180 °C (350 °F) for 30 minutes.
Cook the Monalisa potatoes in the 100% steam oven at 100 °C (210 °F) for 40 minutes. Take the Monalisa potatoes out and give them a quick burst in the oven at 270 °C (520 °F) of dry heat for 5 minutes. Cut in half and smoke with vine shoots for 1 hour.
Smoke the Agria potato skins for 15 minutes.
Liquidise everything in the food processor with the squid ink at 90 °C (195 °F) for 25 minutes. Spread over a Silpat and dry in the dryer for 10 hours.
Mash and sieve twice.

FOR THE FRIED WHITING HEAD AND WHITING BACKBONES

4 whiting heads
4 whiting backbones

Clean the whiting backbones and heads. Put in water and ice for 2 hours.
Dry off and fry in oil at 170 °C (340 °F) for a couple of minutes.

FOR THE WHITING

4 whiting (each 150g)
1L water
30g salt
10g yuzu
10g soy

Clean and fillet the whiting. Put in salted water for 2 hours.
Put the two loins together and roll up in cling film. Leave to rest in the fridge for 12 hours.
Cut the portion, vacuum-wrap and cook for 3 minutes at 56 °C (133 °F) *à la minute*.
Remove the bag wrap and cling film and sear in a hot wok for 5 seconds, adding the soy and yuzu to the wok.

TO FINISH AND PLATE

12 mini maple leaves
4 hake cheeks
50g small capers, fried in oil and left to rest
25g black garlic, finely diced

Sear the hake cheeks on the grill just before serving.

Nicolai Nørregaard.

KADEAU BORNHOLM, COPENHAGEN (DK)

Born in 1979 on the Danish island of Bornholm, Nicolai Nørregaard is the co-founder and head chef of Kadeau in Copenhagen and Kadeau Bornholm. Both restaurants have Michelin stars. As an early proponent of the Nordic Cuisine movement, self-taught Nørregaard is known for his use of pickled and fermented ingredients that make the most of his homeland's produce.

× **What is the story behind the creation of your signature dish?**

NICOLAI NØRREGAARD: *This dish has been with us for years. It's been moderated over time, with various tweaks. Its main particularity is the intense and salty seafood-umami from the mussel liquorice, softened by the slightly stinging horseradish cream. That combined with the soft texture of the raw scallop and the chewy textures of the semi-dried tomatoes and the scallop roe reveals the ultimate tastes of Kadeau.*

× **Where do you come from?**

NICOLAI NØRREGAARD: *I come from Bornholm, a small island in the Baltic Sea and Denmark's easternmost outpost. I grew up with my mum and stepdad living in a small, self-sufficient biodynamic community, where we basically lived in a greenhouse, growing most of our food ourselves. Although it all sounds very nice today, I wasn't fond of it at the time. So, when I grew tired of my mum's vegetarian cooking, I went to my grandparents for some 'normal' food. And there I learned a lot about cooking.*

My grandad was a brilliant cook. He spent his spare time in his garden, in the kitchen or in his little boat catching supper. He inspired me immensely, and planted a seed in me, which became the kitchen philosophy I practise today. He taught me the relevance of great produce and the importance of preservation and building a larder for the cold season, when nothing grows. I owe him a lot.

× **What are your main sources of inspiration?**

NICOLAI NØRREGAARD: *Everything. Shapes, art, colour, nature, architecture, colleagues, co-workers, travelling.*

× **How would you describe your cooking and the philosophy behind it?**

NICOLAI NØRREGAARD: *When we opened Kadeau Bornholm in early 2007, we joined Noma in the exploration of the Nordic kitchen. Back then it was very different from today, and only two or three restaurants had adapted to this philosophy. It meant that there was plenty of unchartered territory, ingredients and techniques to be discovered.*

I wanted to scale it down even further by looking at the whole region to focusing on hyperlocal food, zooming in on the terroirs of my home island of Bornholm. We cook in two seasons: the growing season and the preservation season, meaning that we spend the summer months (May to October) growing, picking and preserving the plants, seeds, nuts and fruits of Bornholm. In the preservation season (October to May) we focus on the larder that we build through summer, and serve Bornholm terroir during the colder and darker months in Kadeau Copenhagen.

× **What are the characteristics of the dishes you like to cook?**

NICOLAI NØRREGAARD: *In my earlier days, I loved cooking very acidic dishes. Fresh and acidic. Today I focus more on texture and balance. Acidity is of course still a factor, but I guess I've become milder and calmer through the years. I guess one of the main characteristics would be aroma, texture and complexity. I often use seafood, and always use plants, berries, nuts or fruits. But at the end of the day, the use of preserves in so many different ways has to be number one.*

× **Does a dish have a calling? And if so, what is it?**

NICOLAI NØRREGAARD: *I wouldn't say so. I sometimes have a sort of epiphany when I get an idea for a dish or a technique, but that's the closest I get!*

× **What are your three favourite ingredients?**

NICOLAI NØRREGAARD: *This isn't set in stone, but at the moment I can't get enough of honey candied figs from our production on Bornholm. I always use figs on the menu; ripe, semi-ripe, unripe and also fig leaves. I also love raw shrimps. Fatty and sweet, preferably with cold cream. Semi-dried tomatoes (in fig leaf oil) are an all-time favourite of mine. Sweet, acidic, intense and flavourful with an amazing chewy texture.*

× **What is your best quality as a chef? And what is your worst?**

NICOLAI NØRREGAARD: *My creativity for sure! And my fault is that I am sometimes a little too ambitious.*

× **What is your main concern: originality or respect for tradition?**

NICOLAI NØRREGAARD: *Both. I think they make a pretty simple marriage.*

× **Which chefs do you admire?**

NICOLAI NØRREGAARD: *The ones that go the extra mile, either by preserving traditions or breaking new ground... and my grandfather, of course.*

NICOLAI NØRREGAARD - KADEAU BORNHOLM

Raw queen scallop, 'mussel liquorice', horseradish cream, chewy tomatoes and blackcurrant wood oil.

SERVES 4

FOR THE SCALLOP

4 live queen scallop, 1 per person

Shuck and rinse the scallop. Slice each scallop vertically in 5 pieces.

FOR THE DRIED SCALLOP ROE

cleaned scallop roe
salt

In a bowl, weigh the scallop roes and season with 2% of the weight in salt. Leave overnight. The next day, mix, seal in a vacuum bag and steam at 63 °C (145 °F) for 1 hour. Chill. Remove from bag and dry until they have a chewy consistency but are not at all hard.

FOR THE SEMI-DRIED TOMATOES

5 small/cherry tomatoes of your choice
blackcurrant wood oil
fig leaf oil
fine salt
sugar

Score the top of the tomatoes. Bring a large pot of water to a boil. Blanch the tomatoes for about 5 seconds. Shock in ice water. Peel the tomatoes and dress with the oils, salt and sugar. Dry at 75 °C (165 °F), turning after a couple of hours. Dry to a chewy, almost leathery consistency.
We harvest our tomatoes from our gardens on Bornholm, we process them as described above and can them in fig leaf oil, so that they keep throughout the winter.

FOR THE HORSERADISH CREAM

100g double cream
20g grated horseradish

Infuse the horseradish in the cream for at least 12 hours. Strain through fishnet.

NICOLAI NØRREGAARD - KADEAU BORNHOLM

FOR THE SCALLOP PASTE

1L mussel stock, highly reduced
scallop powder (powdered dried
scallops)

Reduce the mussel stock until it is quite thick but still liquid. In a Thermomix, add the scallop powder to the stock until a paste is formed.

FOR THE MUSSEL LIQUORICE

20L mussel stock

Slowly reduce the mussel stock until it is almost catching in the pan. During the reduction process change the pan regularly and pass through a fishnet in the early stages while it is still very liquid. Once the stock has almost reached the consistency of a caramel pour it into a small tray lined with silipads.
Bake overnight at 90 °C (195 °F). Cut into pieces and dry in the dehydrator until solid. Store in an airtight box with a Silicasec once completely dry. We call this liquorice because it tastes a bit like raw liquorice.

FOR THE REDUCED BUTTER-
MILK WHEY

1L buttermilk

Bring buttermilk to a boil. When it has split and the curds are set, use a strainer/spider spoon to remove the majority of the curds. Boil again. Pass through a fishnet. Reduce slowly, changing the pan regularly as needed and passing the buttermilk through a double fishnet each time you change the pan. The level of reduction will depend on what you are using it for, but for use as a seasoning, as here, it should be comparable to lemon juice.

TO PLATE

Spread a small dot of scallop paste onto each slice of scallop. Place the scallop pieces in the dried scallop shells, so that they slightly overlap each other.
Marinate the tomatoes in fig leaf oil and a little of the grated mussel liquorice, and plate on top of the scallop pieces.
Slice the dried scallop roe thinly and place on each tomato.
Add 5 drops of buttermilk whey before adding half a spoonful of blackcurrant wood oil and half a spoonful of horseradish cream.
Finish the dish by grating mussel liquorice on top, as seen in the picture.
Fill bowls with ice and place the shells on top and serve.

Junghyun Park.

ATOBOY, NEW YORK (US)

Seoul-born chef Junghyun Park travelled the world from Finland to Australia, before focusing on New Korean cuisine under the guidance of Jungsik Dang while working at his New York outpost. In 2016, he opened Atoboy in New York's NoMad district with his wife Ellia Park. Two years later, the couple launched their equally acclaimed second venture, Atomix, where Park serves a 10-course tasting menu that highlights the best of New Korean cuisine.

× **What is your signature dish, and what does it tell us about you?**

JUNGHYUN PARK: *It's fried chicken with spicy peanut butter and gochujang sauce. This dish represents Atoboy, our first restaurant in New York. It came about while contemplating a menu item that best describes my story: a dish that is as Korean as it is New Yorker, depicting my story of being born and raised in Korea and now living in America. Fried chicken is one of the most popular take-out meals in Korean households whereas peanut butter is very distinctively American.*

× **What is the story behind its creation?**

JUNGHYUN PARK: *I always wanted to make space on our opening menu for a fried chicken that is brined in a spicy marinade. Whilst thinking of its accompanying sauce, peanut butter came to mind with its velvety texture complementing the crispy texture of the fried chicken. I completed this marriage of the Korean and American flavours with elements of spice and fermentation in order to give it a unique and delicious flair. A bit later, the gochujang sauce was introduced to reimagine the classic yangnyum sauce that usually accompanies Korean fried chicken.*

× How would you describe your cooking and the philosophy behind it?

JUNGHYUN PARK: *I think our cooking philosophy starts with Korean cuisine at its core and organically evolves with the changing times and environment to create anew. I want to make sure that the cuisine we create stays fluid by constantly looking for improvements and transformations as needed to contribute to our dining scene.*

× How and when did you become passionate about food?

JUNGHYUN PARK: *I was drawn to food very naturally, always gravitating towards the kitchen since childhood, helping and learning about the art of cooking. My kitchen experience has greatly given me perspective on cooking as a profession, and these days I find gratification in learning and exploring more in-depth the joy that cooking and restaurants bring to people.*

× Which cuisines influenced your cooking?

JUNGHYUN PARK: *Korean cuisine has made the biggest influence on my cooking. Earlier in my career, I was interested in classic French and other western styles of cooking, but as time goes by and my ongoing quest for better food continues, I've become more infatuated with the charm of Korean food. Having said that, I am still very much interested in experiencing different cuisines through my travels and with colleagues around the world.*

× What are the characteristics of the dishes you like to cook?

JUNGHYUN PARK: *I always strive to achieve a balance. Rather than dishes that are bold and extreme in one direction, I gravitate toward dishes that achieve harmony between the ingredients and techniques as well as the different flavours and aroma.*

× Does a dish have a calling? And if so, what is it?

JUNGHYUN PARK: *If I were to choose a dish or a food item that has a calling, I would choose a bowl of freshly cooked white (short-grained) rice. The perfect bowl of rice elevates everything that I love about the complexities of Korean food. Salty brine, savoury fermentation, hearty stews – they are all incomplete without the bowl of rice at the table. In all our three restaurants, rice is a major factor.*

× What are your three favourite ingredients?

JUNGHYUN PARK: *Ganjang (Korean soy sauce), rice, time.*

× What is your main source of inspiration?

JUNGHYUN PARK: *The main source of my inspiration is my travels, meeting new people and experiencing new cultures. New acquaintances and experiences certainly bring inspiration, but I also value a time for self-reflection. The meals during my travels certainly contribute a great deal to the takeaways from each visit. I also find inspiration in cookbooks, online content, art installations and music.*

× What is your main concern: originality or respect for tradition?

JUNGHYUN PARK: *Continued and sustainable improvement. I firmly believe that restaurants must strive to evolve and improve day to day. I am always thinking of how we can build, upon our existing foundations, a better culture to allow for growth and positive improvement overall.*

× Which chefs do you admire?

JUNGHYUN PARK: *Collectively, I admire the new wave of chefs who have recently returned to or have remained in their motherland to widen that region's culture through food. These chefs have not only strengthened their local communities, they have also played a key role in spreading the knowledge of their ingredients, dishes, and techniques to other parts of the world. In a way, these chefs are changing the world; changing the way we see and experience food.*

JUNGHYUN PARK - ATOBOY

Atoboy fried chicken.

SERVES 4

FOR THE CHICKEN

680g boneless, skinless chicken thighs

Portion and trim the chicken thighs into bite-sized pieces or strips.

FOR THE BRINE

1L water
30g salt
70g Yondu vegetable umami
4g onion powder
4g garlic powder

Combine all of the ingredients and mix well. Leave the chicken thighs in the brine for at least 8 hours.

FOR THE FERMENTED JALAPEÑO

543g jalapeño
77g garlic
58g fish sauce
62g sugar
8g salt

Blend all ingredients and let the jalapeño mixture ferment at room temperature for 24 hours.

FOR THE MARINADE

178g garlic
142g pineapple
357g fermented jalapeño
71g ginger

Once the jalapenos have fermented, mix all the marinade ingredients together into a homogenous mixture.
Drain the chicken thighs, then marinate the chicken in the marinade with the fermented jalapeño mixture for another 8 hours.

FOR THE PEANUT BUTTER SAUCE

175g peanut butter (at room temperature)
47g fermented chilli sauce
19g sugar
41g rice vinegar
14g mirin
2g salt
39g water
2g xanthan gum
About 39–55g water

For both sauces, mix each set of the ingredients until smooth (preferably with a blender), and keep refrigerated until ready to enjoy.

FOR THE GOCHUJANG SAUCE

112g gochujang
11g garlic
6g ginger juice
75g tomatoes, tinned
56g corn syrup
41g sugar
37g ketchup
37g water

FOR THE BATTER

1kg Korean fry mix
120g rice flour
80g tapioca
11g xanthan gum

Make the batter by mixing together all the ingredients, adjusting the consistency with water as needed.

TO COOK AND SERVE

Use enough cooking oil for the chicken pieces to be almost fully submerged. Preheat the oil until it reaches 190 °C (375 °F).
Coat the chicken in the batter using tongs and drop gently into the oil. Fry the pieces until fully cooked , 5–10 minutes depending on the size of the chicken pieces.
Serve the chicken with the peanut butter and gochujang sauces.

Christophe Pelé.

LE CLARENCE, PARIS (FR)

Born in 1977 near Paris, Christophe Pelé has worked in many of the capital's Michelin-starred restaurants, from Pierre Gagnaire to Ledoyen. The chef opened his first restaurant in 2007 before launching Le Clarence in 2015. There he celebrates French tradition while weaving in modern thoughts and flavours from all around the world.

—— 'I need a dish to be constantly changing and renewing itself,' explains Christophe Pelé. 'So, I don't have a signature dish at Le Clarence, but for this occasion, I would propose this dish: turbot collar with XO sauce.' This signature dish of sorts features a fish caught in the cold waters of the nearby Atlantic coast, and a spicy sauce originally from Hong Kong.

'The turbot comes from Brittany fished by a Breton woman who practises *ikéjimé* (a Japanese method of killing fish quickly with a spike paralyzing it and draining it from blood to preserve its taste). Her fish have incredible freshness.' And Pelé is also particular about the specific part of the fish he uses, preferring the bottom cheek, because he finds it 'the greediest part of it.'

The turbot cheek is grilled with XO sauce. 'We've been working on our own XO sauce and it has become part of the Le Clarence kitchen now,' explains the chef. His version of the sauce contains traditional dried seafood as well as shiitake mushrooms, Bigorre ham and chorizo. Pelé and his team have used it already to top an oyster wrapped in kadaif; paired it with candied lemon for a dish of sole and calves' intestines; used it to complement a cuttlefish tempura on a slice of kiwi fruit; and even added a splash of it to a squid ink risotto with hazelnut.

Why XO sauce? It must have made a big impression on Pelé during his time in Hong Kong, where he worked as a consultant for a few years, in between closing his first restaurant (a chic bistro called La Bigarrade, which won two Michelin stars and Fooding's Best Chef award) and opening Le Clarence with sommelier Antoine Pétrus four years later. But it all remains a bit of a mystery, as the chef enjoys total freedom when it comes to his sources of inspiration and the creation of his menus.

Pelé's cuisine is not only delicious to eat, it's also bringing new tastes and associations, pushing diners out of their comfort zones, bringing true poetry and audacity on his plates.

CHRISTOPHE PELÉ - LE CLARENCE

Turbot collar with XO sauce.

SERVES 2 - 3

FOR THE XO SAUCE

50g of dried shiitake mushrooms
200g dried scallops
55g dried shrimps
sake and water (equal quantities)
200g soy sauce
1L grapeseed oil
5 shallots, diced
3 or 4 garlic cloves, chopped
some Bigorre black ham and chorizo cut à la brunoise
1 green pepper à la brunoise
20g brown sugar

Put the shiitake, scallops and shrimps in sake and water to hydrate overnight. The next day, steam the scallops for 40 minutes and blend in the mixer.
Cook the shallot in a pan and add the garlic and diced shiitake. Cook for 10 minutes and add the shrimp. Cook for another 15 minutes. Add the scallops. Continue cooking for another 20 minutes.
Add the ham, chorizo and green pepper. Add the soy sauce and the mixture of sake and water used to hydrate the shiitake and scallops. Simmer to reduce.
Mix in the slightly heated oil and add the sugar.

TO FINISH AND PLATE

Prepare the XO sauce with the dried scallops, dried shrimp, Bigorre black ham, the chorizo and sake.
Grill the skin side of the turbot over *binchō-tan* white charcoal for approx. 2 minutes, then grill the another side. Spread the XO sauce on the fish skin side and grill under the salamander. When the sauce starts to caramelise, remove and serve with lightly grilled lime.

Edoardo Pellicano.

(FORMERLY) MAOS, LONDON (UK)

Edoardo Pellicano's dual heritage (his mother is Chinese-Singaporean, his father Italian) informs much of his cooking. The Londoner grew up in his father's Italian restaurant, and followed him to Rome at the age of 14 when he opened a new restaurant there. After returning to London to complete a chef diploma, his first job was at the Michelin-starred Locanda Locatelli, followed by stints at Viajante, Noma, Portland and Mãos.

—— 'My dual Italian and Singaporean background gave me the privilege to taste both eastern and western foods from a very young age, and the flavours from my childhood still greatly inspire me,' says Edoardo Pellicano, whose signature dish, Marco Polo noodles, comprises scallop roe noodles, foie dashi and enoki mushroom floss.

'The dish represents Marco Polo's journey on the Silk Road from Italy to China. His captivating tales introduced one culture to another and greatly influenced society. By combining kombu dashi from Japan, scallop roe from China, and pasta from Italy, we essentially aimed to create something that is cross-cultural,' he explains. 'However, as much as it is about Marco Polo, I also think that this dish largely reflects my own travels; it's the result of taking inspiration from the world and its extensive history.'

Pellicano's dishes – 'simple in presentation but expressive in taste' – are predominantly seafood and vegetable-based. Previous creations include a punchy granita made with kimchi juice; Scottish lobster aged in wild duck fat; and soft-set chocolate with Sakura vinegar and English wasabi. 'Essentially, I would like the dishes to speak for themselves through taste rather than an ornamented display. My cooking aims to explore the best method to portray the optimal flavours and textures of our ingredients.' Among his favourites are a soy sauce from Kisoondo Traditional Jang Farm and pickled green plums from Hongssangri Cheong, both from South Korea; as well as the Fuji Rice Vinegar from Iio Jozo, Japan.

'This dish is in a way a tribute to the ancestors who laid an extraordinary foundation in culinary arts,' says Pellicano, adding: 'There is much yet to learn from the traditions, and through research and experimentation, ancestral knowledge has naturally become my source of inspiration.'

EDOARDO PELLICANO - (FORMERLY) MAOS

Marco Polo noodles.

SERVES 10 (OR 20 TASTING MENU PORTIONS)

FOR THE BROTH

1.5L kombu dashi
90g dried scallop roe
10g dried enoki mushroom
120g foie gras
soy sauce and white soy sauce, to taste

Place the kombu dashi, dried scallop roe and enoki mushroom into a saucepan and bring to the boil, all the while skimming the surface of the stock to remove any scum.
Once boiled, keep the broth hot, but not simmering, for an hour. Then strain the broth by passing it through a muslin cloth.
Bring the temperature up to 85 °C (185 °F) and infuse the foie gras in the stock for 20 minutes. Season with shichimi to taste.
Pass through a muslin cloth again to strain the broth, and finally season with soy sauce and white soy sauce to taste.

FOR THE DRIED ENOKI MUSHROOM FLOSS

dried enoki mushrooms (amount as required)
white soy sauce

Separate the strands of the enoki mushrooms and place them on top of each other to make the desired shape. The amount and shape will vary according to the chosen plating bowls.
Dry the shaped enoki mushrooms at 45 °C (113 °F) overnight or until crispy. Finish by brushing the enoki mushroom floss with white soy sauce.

FOR THE NOODLES
MAKES 390G

137.5g '00' flour
112.5g semolina flour
103g whole eggs
55g egg yolks
20g scallop roe powder
rendered foie gras fat
1 mandarin

Place the '00' flour, semolina flour and scallop roe powder in a stand mixer bowl and mix until evenly combined.
Make a well in the mixture and place the whole eggs and egg yolks in the centre. Fit the stand mixer with the dough hook, start the mixer on low for a few seconds, and then increase the speed to high. Keep mixing until the dough resembles small clusters and comes cleanly off the sides of the bowl. Stop mixing at this point or the dough may dry out.
Take the dough out of the bowl and place it in a vacuum pouch bag. Seal the bag with the vacuum machine at 100% setting. Place the sealed dough in the fridge to rest for at least an hour.
Once rested, take the dough out of the vacuum bag and roll into thick sheets. Run the sheets through a pasta machine on the thickest setting 7 times and fold the sheets between each run through the machine.

Lay the pasta sheets on a gastro tray lined with greaseproof paper. Dry the sheets for 10 minutes on each side in a well-ventilated, cool, dry room. Note that if the sheets dry in a humid room, they will take longer to dry and this, in turn, will affect the noodles' texture.

Dust each side of the sheets with more '00' flour until the exterior of the pasta sheets is dry, but the middle stays pliable. There should be no signs of cracking on the edges of the sheets.

Fold the sheets from the outside in, and cut to the desired thickness.

TO FINISH

Bring salted water up to a boil, then cook the noodles for 45 seconds. Toss the noodles in rendered foie gras fat and place them neatly into a plating bowl.
Use a fine grater (a Japanese zester, if available) to grate a small amount of mandarin zest on top of the noodles.
Once the noodles are ready, heat the broth to a simmer and pour it into the bowl.
Place the dried enoki floss on top to finish.

Dave Pynt.

BURNT ENDS, SINGAPORE (SG)

Originally from Perth, Dave Pynt is a Noma and St John alumnus. He is the chef patron of the Michelin-starred Burnt Ends, opened in 2013 in Singapore and a chain of barbecue restaurants, Meatsmith.

—— 'There is nothing better than freshly grilled seafood,' says Australian chef Dave Pynt, and we're more than ready to believe him, given his sensational signature dish. It features Western Australian marron — a large freshwater crayfish — as well as flying fish roe and smoked beurre blanc. 'This dish tells you that I am from Western Australia. I love fresh seafood and wood-fired cooking.'

After being trained with chefs known for their elaborate, time-consuming processes and hyper-refined dishes ('chefs such as Tetsuya Wakuda, Bittor Arginzoniz, René Redzepi, Fergus Henderson and Nuno Mendes have all played a big part in shaping my philosophy', the chef says), Pynt likes to keep things simple, at least in terms of explaining his culinary approach: 'We like to BBQ — simple big flavours and great technique.'

'I love to cook large format dishes, especially those that take a longer time to cook.' For Pynt, 'dishes should be a pleasure to eat, and not require thought to enjoy.' Burnt Ends is first and foremost 'a modern Australian barbecue restaurant' and his favourite ingredients are fire, dairy and vegetables, respectively. At the heart of Burnt Ends, recently relocated in Dempsey Hills in Singapore, is an open-concept kitchen with a custom four-tonne oven and four elevation grills. Appearing on one of Raymond Blanc's TV shows a few years ago, Pynt famously told the French-British chef: 'First, we need to burn the shit out of the leek.'

Today the chef remains as straight-talking as ever, especially when talking about feeling the heat in the kitchen, and Burnt Ends has been dubbed 'all smoke and no mirrors': 'This is a hard job that you can only do successfully if you dive in head first. Anyone that commits to being a chef long term deserves my admiration.' Pynt is definitely in it for the long haul, having moved Burnt Ends to a much larger location, where he added a stunning chef's table, a bar and a bakery to the project.

DAVE PYNT - BURNT ENDS

Western Australian marron with tobiko and kombu beurre blanc.

SERVES 5 - 10

FOR THE MARRON

5 whole live marron (Western Australian freshwater crayfish), split in half and claws separated
1L vegetable oil

Put the claws into a preheated oven at 250 °C (480 °F) for 6 minutes. Preheat the vegetable oil until the temperature reaches 180 °C (355 °F). Place the half marron, shell side down, under the grill, and grill until the internal temperature reaches 35 °C (95 °F).
Remove the half marron and place on a shallow 50mm gastro tray. Carefully pour the hot vegetable oil over the marron to finish the cooking. Drain off the excess oil and arrange beautifully on the plate.
Remove the claws from the oven and use to recreate the marron. Fill the marron with the beurre blanc and garnish with fresh chives.

FOR THE TOBIKO AND KOMBU BEURRE BLANC

30g banana shallot, peeled and julienned
8 black peppercorns
1 bay leaf
150ml dry white wine
75ml UHT cream
250g smoked butter, cut into small dice
35g tobiko (flying fish roe)
15g dried kombu, minced
chives, freshly chopped, to garnish
Maldon sea salt
fresh lemon juice

Put the shallots, bay leaf, black peppercorns and white wine into a saucepan, and reduce until syrupy. Add the cream and bring to the boil. Then allow to cool to room temperature. Now start adding the butter, slowly whisking. Keep whisking until all the butter has been absorbed.
Slowly heat up and strain out the aromatics. Then finish the sauce with the tobiko and kombu. Adjust the seasoning with Maldon salt and lemon juice.

TO PLATE

Serve the marron with jugs of the sauce to one side.

Emmanuel Renaut.

FLOCONS DE SEL, MEGÈVE (FR)

Born in 1968 in northern France, Emmanuel Renaut founded his restaurant Flocons de Sel in Megève in 1998 after stints at Marc Veyrat's Auberge and Claridges in London. He received his first Michelin star in 2003, a second in 2006, and a third in 2012.

—— Renaut's signature dish, croûte de fromage (cheese on toast) with wild mushroom, was partly inspired by the French Alps, which he fell in love with while on a skiing trip in Haute-Savoie as a child. 'This dish talks about our direct connection with nature,' explains Renaut. 'As always, we highlight the local products of our mountains, thanks to the wild mushroom and cheeses sourced from our splendid area.'

The adopted Savoyard couldn't be a better ambassador for the mountainous department: 'Our cuisine represents our region, through our producers, fishermen, fruit pickers...' As for the croûte of fromage, it features Beaufort as its star ingredient, an Alpine cheese similar to Swiss Gruyère but originating from Savoie's Beaufortain, Tarentaise and Maurienne valleys. On the menu at Flocons de Sel there are plenty of other mountain pasture cheeses, including Reblochon, Abondance, bleu de Termignon and Tomme. To select these cheeses, Renaut works in close collaboration with Jacques Dubouloz, an award-winning local cheese specialist who is his 'eyes in the mountains'.

Renaut credits his first real encounter with fine dining to Le Crillion ('this is where I really started to learn to cook'), while his passion for local produce — his favourites are mushrooms, freshwater fish from the lakes and wild herbs — was inspired by working for seven years with Marc Veyrat, an early proponent of molecular gastronomy, renowned for his use of roots, mountain plants, mountain herbs and wild flowers harvested in the French Alps.
Other key influences are the work of the great Paul Bocuse and Joël Robuchon, as well as the master pâtissier and chocolatier Yves Thuriès, with whom Renaut briefly worked.

Now perfectly settled in Megève with his award-winning restaurant, hotel and spa, Renault continues his search for new culinary heights.

EMMANUEL RENAUT - FLOCONS DE SEL

Wild mushrooms with a baked cheese crust.

SERVES 4

FOR THE FERMENTED PORCINI JUICE (PREPARE 72 HOURS IN ADVANCE)

2kg frozen porcini mushrooms
40g fine salt

Put the porcini mushrooms and salt in a large, vacuum-sealed bag. Leave to ferment for 3 days, then strain.
Preheat the oven to 170 °C (340 °F).

FOR THE CARAMELISED ONIONS

3 yellow onions
30g butter
salt and sugar

Slice the onions and brown in a pan with a tablespoon of butter. Sauté until golden brown, then add a pinch of sugar to caramelise them. Chop finely.

FOR THE SIPHON MIX

2 eggs
2 egg yolks
160g clarified butter
100g fresh butter
75g fermented porcini juice

Warm the butters, then mix the egg yolks and whole eggs together in a large pot. Stir the warm butter in over the eggs. Season with fermented porcini juice and salt.
Place the mixture in a syphon and keep warm.

FOR THE CRUST

100g butter
50g sugar
120g egg white
100g flour
10g fine salt

Mix the ingredients and spread out on the moulds. Bake in the oven for about 10 minutes.

FOR THE MUSHROOMS

50g chanterelles
50g oyster mushrooms
50g mousserons (fairy ring mushrooms)
50g trumpet mushrooms
25g fermented porcini juice
hazelnut oil to taste
chopped parsley to taste

Chop the onions into large cubes and pan-fry. Once cooked, deglaze with a little fermented porcini juice, then add the parsley.

TO PLATE

20g diced Beaufort cheese
caramelised hazelnuts to taste

In a bowl, arrange a small spoonful of caramelised onions and add the pan-fried mushrooms. Add 5 or 6 cubes of Beaufort cheese on top, a few caramelised hazelnuts and a few drops of hazelnut oil. Top with a little of the syphon mix.
To finish, gently place the crust on top.

SIGNATURE DISHES — 197

Joan Roca.

EL CELLER DE CAN ROCA, GIRONA (ES)

The Roca brothers opened El Celler de Can Roca in 1996 next to their parents' restaurant Can Roca in Girona. Joan is the head chef; Josep, the sommelier; and Jordi is in charge of desserts. Constantly pushing the boundaries of technique and flavour, El Celler has twice been named the best restaurant in the world, in 2013 and 2015.

— Joan, Josep and Jordi Roca chose their soil and oyster dish as their signature creation for one reason: it's a typical Catalan dish combining ingredients from the land and sea in a radical way. 'This is surf and turf taken to its most minimalist end,' they say, 'and it represents the gastronomic tradition of Catalonia.'

Originally created in 2006, the dish features as its star component petrichor, the pleasant smell that frequently accompanies the first rain after a long period of warm, dry weather. 'We trap the aroma of petrichor in a distillate version of the soil,' explains Joan. In order to trap this particular scent, the team distils soil in a Rotaval at low temperature. This piece of equipment (created in 2005 by the brothers in collaboration with Fundación Alicia) removes air during distillation, allowing very clean, clear and concise distillation of flavours.

The resulting extract 'provides an earthy sensation without precedent, a magnificent mildness that combines with the oceanic sensation of the oyster.' It's then thickened with Xanthan gum and poured over a fresh oyster. A Catalan speciality, the shellfish is a particular favourite at El Celler, in dishes such as freeze-dried oyster shell with oyster tartare, oyster with melon granita, or oyster with fennel sauce and sea anemone.

Distillation is one of the many techniques used at El Celler, where chefs are busy exploring the possibilities offered by sous-vide broths, fermentation or reimagining ancestral recipes with added magic. One of Jordi's passions is analysing different perfumes, so the team can create dishes from the notes they discover. As well as soil, they have attempted to extract the essence of a myriad of unusual items, from antique books to sheep's wool.

All this research takes place at La Masia, a cutting-edge lab set within a traditional Catalan house from 1898, a stone's throw from the restaurant. Dubbed the I&R centre ('I' for innovation, investigation, ideation, imagination and 'R' for Roca, recreation, risk, renovation roots, reflection'), it also has a room dedicated to creating a new 'Roca spirit', using Catalan plants, fermented ingredients, extraction of essential oils and the distillation of products such as the regional Pals rice.

JOAN ROCA - EL CELLER DE CAN ROCA

Soil and oyster.

SERVES 4

FOR THE OYSTERS

4 oysters

Open the oysters and remove them from their shell without damaging them. Remove the beard with a pairing knife and reserve refrigerated until plating.

FOR THE SOIL DISTILLATE
(YIELDS 430G)

300g soil
500g water
0.2g xanthan gum
salt

Mix the soil and water, cover the container and infuse for 12 hours refrigerated. Introduce the infusion in the evaporating flask with a 0.22μm sterilisation membrane filter between the flask and the outlet towards the cooler. Distil the soil at 30–35°C (86–95°F) (bath temperature) for 1–2 hours, and finish at 40–45 °C (104–113 °F) for 30 minutes. Remove the distillate and seal it in a vacuum pack bag to conserve its aroma. To keep the distillate for days or weeks, freezing is recommended.

TO PLATE

Thicken the distillate with xanthan gum and adjust salt.
Place the oyster in the middle of the plate and pour soil distillate on it.

João Rodrigues.

MATÉRIA, LISBON (PT)

Born in Lisbon, João Rodrigues was at the helm of the city's Michelin-starred Feitoria from 2013 to 2022. He is the founder of Matéria, a non-profit project that promotes environmentally friendly agricultural practices in Portugal.

—— Portuguese chef João Rodrigues believes that 'there is a connection between food and several other disciplines. And that identity is conveyed in many forms.' He aims to express his own experiences through food, focusing on 'things that touch me somehow,' including 'other people, architecture, travels, nature, the sea, art, and life itself.' One such thing is the work of Amadeo de Sousa Cardoso, a Portuguese painter, whose modernist, geometric artworks were the inspiration for Rodrigues' signature dish.

'This dish was inspired by the work of the avant-garde painter from the early 20th century who at the start of his career painted only in black and white,' explains Rodrigues. 'So, I looked for very round shapes, curled in themselves, and of course only in black and white, like a complexed simplicity.' To do this, the chef used poached hake, grilled squid tagliatelle with sheep butter sauce and Vinho Verde sauce. Rodrigues, who is a fan of Thomas Keller and Alain Senderens, and has fond memories of working for Fausto Airoldi and Sebastien Grospelier, says intuition tells him when a dish is complete: 'For me it's quite a natural thing, I can't explain it, it just feels right… And when it does, it's an addictive and marvellous feeling.'

The chef says three cuisines in particular have informed his work: French, for its techniques and flavours; Japanese, for its respect for products and aesthetics; and Portuguese, for its flavour, identity and drive. 'I like the idea of Portuguese cuisine as a traveller's cuisine,' he says. 'Most of the products we use are not from here: tomato originally is from China; peppers, potatoes, corn and coriander from South America; almonds and sugar from North Africa; codfish from the northern seas, and so forth.'

Rodrigues describes his cooking style as 'looking for seasonality and local products, empathy with nature, and at the same time influenced by travelling and other cultures.' His passion for products comes directly from his father, a keen hunter, fisherman and cook. 'I grew up with all these products and flavours,' he says. 'I remember going to the open market with him and touching all these different products; the textures, the colours. It was one of my favourite things when I was a kid.'

JOÃO RODRIGUES - MATÉRIA

Squid with sheep's butter and chives.

SERVES 1

FOR THE SQUID

1 squid of 90g, cleaned
fleur du sel
1 tbsp olive oil

Season the squid with salt and olive oil and quickly cook on a hot skillet, so that the squid gets a nice golden colour on the outside but remains juicy and tender on the inside.

FOR THE SAUCE

1 tsp water
a little lemon juice
250g sheep's butter, cubed, set aside to cool
chives, finely chopped

Heat a pan with the water and the lemon juice until it boils. Turn down the heat to a minimum and gradually add the butter, whisking constantly. Continue until there is no butter remaining and you have obtained a dense, glossy butter sauce. Finish with chopped chives.

Serve the sauce immediately over the grilled squid.

Julien Royer.

ODETTE, SINGAPORE (SG)

Born in central France in 1982 to fourth-generation farmers, Julien Royer is the chef-owner of Odette and Claudine in Singapore and Louise in Hong Kong. In 2019 and 2020, Odette was named number 1 on Asia's 50 Best List, and awarded the highest distinction of three stars by the Michelin guide.

— 'Pigeon is one of my favourite meats to work with and it's something I grew up eating,' says chef Julien Royer of his signature dish. 'The pigeon is cooked on the bone and crusted with a special pepper sourced from the Kampot Jewel farm in Cambodia, run by my longtime friend, Norbert Binot. The pepper in this recipe imparts a distinctive fragrance and spice with a long-lasting finish. I was drawn to its distinctive profile — an intense spiciness, yet a mild sweetness and a delicate aroma. We thought it would work very well as a crust against tender juicy game meat, so we tried many different versions of this to achieve the right complexity and contrast of flavours.'

'We try to use every single part of the pigeon so nothing is left to waste,' continues the French chef. 'It's prepared in various ways, showcasing the many facets of flavour and texture within: a confit leg, a pan-seared breast, a pigeon liver parfait, barbecued pigeon heart tempura, and a heart or liver samosa gyoza.'

Named after Royer's grandmother ('a fantastic cook who showed me how much pleasure, joy, happiness and emotion you can give to people through food'), Odette is a true melting pot. 'Our cuisine remains French in its DNA, and over the years we've consistently infused a sense of place, which is at the crossroads of Southeast Asia, through product, technique, aesthetics and flavours. We source our ingredients from boutique producers around the world — from farms right here in Singapore and Asia, to explore a variety of native spices and citrus across the region.'

Royer's mentors include Bernard Andrieux, with whom he learned the DNA of French cuisine, Alain Passard and Michel Bras. 'Michel opened my mind and instilled in me a deep respect for the integrity and purity of each ingredient in every dish,' says Royer. 'Ingredients are a reflection of the land and I always believe in working with produce in season when it's at the peak of its quality. If I have to name one favourite ingredient, I would say citrus. When I moved to Asia, I discovered many rare varieties of citrus — the variety here is simply amazing! I love how it adds a bright freshness to any dish and in some instances, a sense of finesse and complexity.'

JULIEN ROYER - ODETTE

Kampot pepper–crusted pigeon.

SERVES 6

FOR THE PEPPER CRUST

23g black Kampot pepper
150g butter
100g breadcrumbs

Melt the butter. Blend the pepper and breadcrumbs, separately, until fine. Once the butter is melted, add the pepper and cook gently for 2 minutes. After that, whisk in the breadcrumbs until incorporated. Transfer to a container and cool down at room temperature.
Once cool, spread some of the crust between 2 pieces of baking paper and spread thinly with a rolling pin – it should not be thicker than 2mm. Freeze the sheet, then remove one side of the parchment paper. Using a teardrop mould, punch out the pepper crust and store between sheets of baking paper in the fridge.

FOR THE PIGEON

3 pigeons, fresh if possible, legs with the whole foot on
100g duck fat
Salt, to taste

Remove the head and wings with a pair of scissors. Discard the head and save the wings for the sauce. Use a knife to remove the leg, then trim off all the claws except for the middle one. Blanch the claw of the leg in boiling water, then pull the skin off the claw, using a cloth for tension if required. Salt the legs lightly, then lay them out in a vacuum bag in a flat layer. Add 75g duck fat to the bag, then seal fully. Cook the legs at 70 °C (158 °F) for 5 hours, then cool down quickly in ice.
Remove the backbone of the pigeon using a pair of scissors, saving it for making the jus. Remove the wishbone of the pigeon. Keep the breast of the pigeon on the crown in the fridge until needed. Sear the pigeon straight from the fridge on the skin side until well coloured all around.
Temper at room temperature for 25 minutes, then finish in the oven at 160 °C (320 °F) for about 3–5 minutes, looking to reach a core temperature of around 52–55 °C (125–131 °F), then letting it rest until it reaches a core temperature of 58–60 °C (136–140 °F).
Carve the breasts off the frame of the pigeon, then place a piece of the crust on the skin side. Warm up under a heat lamp until the crust is melted, then cut in half lengthwise, trimming the sides so that the breast sits on the plate with the cut side facing up.
For the legs, sear the skin side in the remaining duck fat, pressing down lightly to ensure a crispy skin.

FOR THE ALMOND PASTE

500g almonds with skins still on
100g almond oil

Bake the almonds at 180 °C (355 °F) for 8–9 minutes – they should smell roasted and nutty. Blend immediately in a Thermomix at full speed, for at least 3 minutes, adding the almond oil in the last 30 seconds.

FOR THE BARLEY RISOTTO

500g barley
2 sprigs thyme
1 bay leaf
2 banana shallots, finely chopped
200ml white wine
1L chicken stock

Sweat the shallots in olive oil. Add in barley and herbs and cook for a few minutes to infuse the herbs. Deglaze with the white wine and reduce until almost dry. Add enough chicken stock to cover the barley, then bring to a simmer. Repeat 3–4 times with the remaining stock – the barley should be fully cooked.
To finish, fold in some of the almond paste and adjust with more chicken stock to a creamy consistency. It should resemble a regular risotto. Season to taste with salt and a small amount of freshly ground black pepper.

FOR THE PIGEON JUS

750g brown onions, sliced
500g butter
300g garlic, halved
200 pigeon frames
10kg chicken stock

Roast the pigeon bones in the oven at 200 °C (390 °F) until nicely browned. Sauce the onions and garlic in a large pot with the butter until golden. Add in the chicken stock and roasted pigeon bones and simmer for 4 hours. Strain the pigeon stock, remove as much of the fat as possible, then reduce to a jus consistency. Add a small amount of amaretto liquor to the jus, just before serving.

FOR THE BLACK GARLIC PURÉE

1kg black garlic
500g mirin
3 banana shallots
250g sherry vinegar
xanthan gum

Sweat shallots in olive oil until translucent. Add black garlic, sherry vinegar and mirin, and continue to simmer to soften the black garlic. In a Thermomix, blend until very smooth, adding a small amount of xanthan gum to obtain a glossy and thick purée (we usually add it in 0.2g increments, blending 30 seconds between each addition).

FOR THE PICKLED ONIONS

1kg red pearl onions
300g sugar
600g red wine vinegar
900g water

Cut all the onions into half. Combine the remaining ingredients and bring to a boil. Pour the hot pickling liquid over the onions, cover with a layer of plastic wrap, then leave to cool at room temperature. Chill overnight, then separate into petals, cutting the larger ones into half if necessary.

FOR THE GLAZED CHERRIES

sherry vinegar, to deglaze
small amount of sugar
3 cherries, cut in half, seeds removed

Place a sauté pan on medium-high heat, then sear the cherries, cut side down, with a pinch of sugar. Once the sugar has liquefied, deglaze with the vinegar and cook it down quickly to a glaze. Remove the cherries immediately once they are glossy and shiny.

FOR THE DUMPLING FARCE

600g chicken thigh
300g foie gras, tempered at room temperature
48g truffle paste
10g thyme (leaves plucked)
50g soy sauce
30g Shiro dashi
salt, to taste
gyoza skins

Vacuum-seal the chicken thighs with a bit of salt, duck fat, thyme, bay leaf and garlic. Cook at 85 °C (185 °F) for 2 hours, then chill in an ice bath. Cut into small chunks. Mix it with the rest of the ingredients in a large bowl until well incorporated.

Punch out the gyoza skins with a large ring mould. Place 4g of the farce into the centre and wrap the gyoza, applying water to the rim of the dumping skin to stick them together. Crimp one side of the dumpling skin, making 7 folds in total.

Add some oil to a pan and cook the dumplings on their flat side until crispy and golden brown. Turn off the heat, deglaze with a small amount of water and cover the pan with a lid. Turn the heat back on and leave to cook until fully cooked. Remove the lid and continue to cook the dumpling until the seared side is crispy.

Ana Roš.

HIŠA FRANKO, KOBARID (SI)

Born in 1972, Ana Roš is a self-taught Slovenian chef who took over her parents' restaurant, Hiša Franko in the Soča Valley, after completing her diplomacy studies. Named the World's Best Female Chef in 2017, she currently has two Michelin stars.

—— A nod to Slovenian Sunday lunches, in which a piece of meat is slowly roasted with carrots, onions and white wine, Roš's signature dish, called 'Where is the meat?', brings a twist to the traditional dish. As its name makes clear, there is no actual meat in the creation. Yet it's far from a vegetarian dish, as it uses the offcuts from other, meatier dishes on Hiša Franko's menu.

'This main course doesn't contain a piece of meat, but nestling in the cooked onion you will find a sauce that we cook from all the leftovers: lamb, pork, beef,' explains the chef. 'The sauce is cooked for a few days with a lot of aromatic herbs.' This includes bay leaves, lemon thyme and fresh oregano, which Roš grows in her sprawling kitchen garden.

Sustainability, farm-to-table and zero-kilometre sourcing are all part of the traditional rural Slovenian lifestyle, but the kitchen garden and close relationship with local producers was also a necessity for Roš. There were no suppliers in her remote Soča Valley location, so she had to improvise to get ingredients, building relationships with local farmers and foragers. The former supply her with goat and rabbit meat, while the latter scour the forests for wild strawberries, edible flowers and mushrooms. 'Where is the meat?' also features a mushroom wrap, with porcini purée and salad, and is served with a linden leaf on the side.

'All these elements are served on a reinterpretation of the Ethiopian injera, a "thousand-hole" fermented flatbread,' explains Roš. 'It's made with roasted barley, along with dark malted barley oil.' This unexpected element represents what the Slovenian chef has called her 'big creative twist', and is typical of her distinctive approach.

'When you eat my food, you always get explosions of flavours,' she once said. 'You have all the senses working all the time. This is a kitchen with guts. You might hear some people say they didn't like it, but you'll never hear anyone say it was forgettable.'

ANA ROŠ - HIŠA FRANKO

Where is the meat?

Injera of roasted barley flour and dark malted barley oil, onion, lamb, chicken, pork offcuts stock, celeriac, preserved berries, king oyster mushrooms, toasted hazelnuts

SERVES 4

FOR THE DARK MALT OIL

900g malt powder
621g rapeseed oil
9g sugar
15.5g salt

Combine all ingredients in the *conchadora* (conching machine) and proccess for 2 hours. Reserve in a plastic container until needed.

FOR THE INJERA BREAD

250g all-purpose flour
13.5g salt
125g sourdough starter
250g dark malt oil
500g water

Combine all ingredients in a plastic container and mix well using a hand blender. Allow to ferment overnight at room temperature before using.

FOR THE CHICKEN STOCK BASE

20g garlic peeled
140g white onion, sliced on a mandoline
160g parsnip, sliced on a mandoline
150g fennel bulb, sliced on a mandoline
325g chicken back bone and breast
30g fennel seeds
0.25g cloves
20g fresh bay leaves with stalk
5g oregano fresh
5g cinammon stick
45g rapeseed oil
50ml water
1.5L water

Brown the garlic in the oil on all sides. Fry the bones in the same oil on all sides, until you get a nice caramelised colour. Add all the spices and briefly roast.
Take everything out of the pan, add the finely sliced vegetables and brown them. Add a little water if neccesary to deglaze the pan.
Mix the spiced bones, vegetables and the rest of the ingredients and pour over 1.5L water. Simmer for 2–3 hours.

PORK STOCK

800g pork bones (chopped into 5cm pieces)
10g garlic
30g rapeseed oil
100g dried pears
27g fresh bay leaves on their stalks
25g fresh oregano
90g butter
4g salt
5g sugar
900ml chicken stock
400ml water

Brown the garlic in the oil on all sides. Fry the bones in the same oil on all sides, until you get a nice caramelised colour. Add all the spices and briefly roast together with the butter, this will make a nice and caramelised bones together with the dry pears.
Take everything out of the pan, add the thinly sliced vegetables and brown them, following the same steps used to make the chicken stock.
Mix all the ingredients together and pour over the previously made chicken stock. Simmer for 2–3 hours.

FOR THE LAMB JUS

270g white onion (aprox. 2 onions, each cut in half)
27g garlic
150g dry red wine
150g port
150g white wine
550g lamb neck with bone
60g rapeseed oil (30g + 30g)
100g butter
20g fresh bay leaves on their stalks
50g fresh oregano
salt
pork stock

Brown the garlic in the oil on all sides. Fry the bones in the same oil on all sides, until you get a nice caramelised colour. Add all the spices and briefly roast.
Take everything out of the pan, add the thinly sliced vegetables and brown them. Deglaze with the wines and then put the lamb meat back into the pan.
Mix all ingredients and pour over the previously made chicken and pork stocks. Simmer for 2–3 hours. Through the cooking process, add oregano and bay leaves at least three times, removing the used herbs before putting in the fresh ones.

NOTE: It is very important to use fresh oregano and bay leaves. Avoid using dried ones.

FOR THE ONION SHELLS

4 yellow onions (110g each)
50g butter in dises
4g fresh bay leaves
4g fresh oregano
4g lemon thyme
100g vegetable oil
100g dry red wine
100g dry white wine
100g port

Take a pot and heat up the oil. Cut the onions in half and place them flat side down in the pan. Make sure the rondón is hot so the onions get a nice dark colour. Flip the onions over and cook on the curved side, sprinkling some salt on top of the flat side, then flip again, so that the flat side is facing down again. Now add the butter and aromatics, whisk to foam the butter, add the wines and reduce. Once the alcohol is gone, take the pan off the heat and allow the onions to cool. Separate the onion out into individual petals – you should get about 7–8 portions out of one whole onion.

FOR THE PORCINI PURÉE

300g porcini
15g garlic
150g white onion
40g butter
3g savory plus 3g more for the Thermomix
12g salt
100g mushroom broth
2g gelespessa
2g black pepper
20g olive oil

Roast the garlic with the olive oil and remove the garlic. Add the onion and roast. Add the porcini and roast. Add the mushroom broth and the savory, then cook for 2 minutes.
Finally, add the salt and the roasted garlic, then put everything in the Thermomix with the gelespessa and mix at 70 °C (160 °F) for 3 minutes. As the final step, add the fresh savory and black pepper and mix for another minute.

FOR THE PORCINI SALAD

200g porcini mushrooms
50g olive oil plus extra for dressing
chilli flakes
salt

Cut the porcini in dices and cook thoroughly in hot olive oil, being careful not to allow the pan to get too hot, as this will give a bitter note to the mushrooms as well as spoiling the texture. Season the mushrooms with olive oil, salt, black pepper and chilli. The spicy note should be gentle but present. Reserve.

ELDERBERRIES

500g apple vinegar
150g elderflower

Combine the vinegar and elderflower, and cook sous vide' at 65 °C (150 °F) for 2 hours. Allow to cool down and infuse for at least 1 week before using.

FOR THE ELDERBERRIY DRESSING

500g elderflower vinegar
250g elderflower syrup
350g elderberries

Combine all the ingredients in a pan and reduce by two-thirds, and reserve. At Hiša Franko, we use the leaf of either the linden tree or Sicilian serpent squash. Cut the leaves with a 7cm cutter, and then place a thick line of them at the bottom of the purée, then on top the porcini mushrooms, and finally some berries on top as well. Close up and reserve ready for serving.

FOR THE ROASTED HAZELNUTS

500g hazelnuts

Cut the hazelnuts in half, place in a flat tray and toast them in the oven at 175 °C (350 °F) for 10 minutes. Set aside.

TO PLATE

Take a fresh lipa (lindl leaf) and with a pipping bag, put about 5g of porcini purée, on top of the purée add between 7-8g of porcini salad, and dinally a bit of the elderberries. Put a bit of the porcini purée on the side of the leaf, in order to be able to close it. Keep aside.
On top of the injera right side, place the lipa leaf taco, on the left side place the onion shell and inside of it place the 3 meats jus, to the top, add 2 halves of toasted hazelnuts on top of the jus.

Prateek Sadhu.

(FORMERLY) MASQUE, MUMBAI (IN)

Born in Kashmir in 1986, Prateek Sadhu graduated from the Culinary Institute of America with double gold medals, and worked in some of the world's finest kitchens, including The French Laundry, Noma and Alinea. He was the executive chef and co-owner of Masque in Mumbai from 2016 to 2022.

—— 'Many dishes have a special meaning to me, but if I have to pick one, it would be the smoked mackerel on toast,' says Prateek Sadhu. The main reason for this choice is that it incorporates a tradition from his beloved home state of Kashmir.

'Since winters are harsh in Kashmir, there are many preservation techniques to take inspiration from, explains Sadhu. 'One of them is called "fherigaad", and it's a real winter delicacy. The fish is laid out to dry for a day, then spread over dry grass, which is torched to smoke the fish evenly. It's one of the oldest methods of preservation, used long before refrigerators. The crispy skin is scraped off before it's cooked with vegetables.'

Here, it is used to prepare mackerel, which is served with a garlic-chilli spread on buckwheat toast. Buckwheat used to be a staple food for the people of Ladakh and Kashmir, but its production has declined in recent years, partly because of its high sensitivity to climate as well as growing competition with newer crops such as wheat and French beans.

'My cooking style is very rooted in Indian cooking traditions,' says the chef. 'To me, the future of Indian food begins with us taking a look back at everything that came before us, and understanding those techniques and traditions, then building upon them.' He continues: 'It begins with the right vocabulary to define the dishes, and attributing the source to authenticity, ensuring that the food, or the community behind it, isn't exoticised or othered in the process. Their stories should be effortlessly woven into the larger whole.'

Sadhu who grew up around family farms and learned the basics of the kitchen from his aunt and mother, trained in America and worked in top restaurants including The French Laundry, Alinea and Noma. He opened Masque with a clear focus on ingredient-led dishes, using produce from his mountainous home state, such as walnuts, pumpkins and lotus stems. Some of the dishes the chef has cooked up include lamb brain paniyaram, turmeric scampi, sweet potato paniyaram, morel and gutti aloo, and a dessert of rich Pondicherry chocolate served with a sprinkle of edible ants.

After leaving Masque in 2022, Sadhu is now travelling the world, looking for new food and inspiration, and collaborating at pop-up events along the way.

PRATEEK SADHU - (FORMERLY) MASQUE

Unicorn Pani Puri.

SERVES 6

FOR THE PANI PURI

200g sooji (semolina)
45g refined oil
180ml hot water
a pinch of salt

Mix the sooji (semolina) and oil gently in a bowl. Add the hot water, wait for a minute, then knead the mixture until it forms a dough. Rest the dough for 30 minutes.
Knead the dough again to develop the gluten, then roll using a rolling pin to 1mm thickness.
Cut the puris with a disc cutter and fry on a high to medium flame until the puris puff up.
Alternatively, the puris can be cooked over embers.

FOR THE CORN FOAM

2 whole corn on the cob
100g unsalted butter
2g salt
100ml double cream
100ml whole milk
5ml apple cider vinegar

Peel the corn on the cob and remove the corn from the cob using a knife.
Add the butter and salt to a saucepan and slowly sweat the corn, keeping the lid on and stirring periodically.
Remove from the flame and add the milk and cream, then blend the mixture until the consistency is silky smooth. Add the vinegar and pass through a chinois.
Add the mixture to a syphon and double charge.

FOR THE KALE GEL

40g kale leaves (stalks removed)
1 green apple
40g coriander leaves
2 green chilis
15ml lemon juice
3g xanthan gum
2g salt
2g black salt
3g granulated sugar
4–5 ice cubes

Wash the kale leaves, coriander leaves and green apple. Roughly chop the kale leaves and coriander leaves, and finely dice the apple.
Add to a juicer together with the xanthan gum, lemon, salts and ice cubes and blend until smooth.

TO SERVE

Take a puri and make a small hole. Add corn foam until it is almost full, then add kale gel on top of the foam the hole is covered. Add a generous amount of sea urchin, then place a dollop of caviar on top.
Each puri is enough for one bite only.

Eyal Shani.

HASALON, NEW YORK (US)

Born in Jerusalem in 1959, Eyal Shani is a world famous icon of Israeli cuisine. He opened his first restaurant, Oceanus, in his hometown in 1989. Since the launch of his fine-dining restaurant HaSalon in Tel Aviv in 2018, Shani has branched out with 40 highly successful restaurants worldwide.

—— Eyal Shani's passion was first instilled in him by his grandfather, an agronomist and dedicated vegan, who exposed him to local markets, fields and vineyards from a young age. This is how he was taught to believe in the power of ingredients: 'My job is to convert raw materials —mostly vegetables — into a dish where they become the star,' he says. 'I'm writing a culinary sentence, and my subjects are mainly olive oil, sea salt and the ingredient itself. I don't really use spices.' The chef's famous whole roasted cauliflower is a case in point.

Shani boils the whole head for a few minutes in hot water, roasts it in the oven until it turns golden brown, and finishes it with a dose of coarse sea salt from the Atlantic Ocean, which he says adds a sweetness to any dish.

Truly passionate about his key ingredients, the chef believes in the necessity to keep it all in one piece. 'The cauliflower was once a cabbage — so was broccoli, kohlrabi and brussels sprouts. About 5,000 years ago, man domesticated cabbage and chose the specimens with the biggest flowers to hybridise. This gave birth to a cabbage that is almost a flower: the cauliflower,' he explains. 'Since then, throughout ages, cultures, and cuisines, people mistakenly saw it as a bouquet of cauliflowers, so they break it down into tiny flower fragments. I believe it's like taking a flower, tearing its petals apart and claiming that each of them is a flower. That is why I decided never to break apart any more flowers of our roasted cauliflower.'

This signature dish is illustrating the essence of my cuisine: to turn raw ingredients into a dish where it becomes the star. I boil the whole head of the cauliflower for a few minutes in hot water and roast it in the oven until it turns golden brown. I finish it with a dose of coarse sea salt from the Atlantic Ocean, which adds a sweetness to any dish. As the secrets of cooking are often found within the movements of the body, I found myself caressing the cauliflower with both hands. This is how I found the exact amount of olive oil needed: it is exactly the amount gathered by two palms of hands, bathed in oil.'

In the kitchen, Shani instructs his chefs: 'You're working from intuition, taking a big risk, you're not trying to be safe, you're on a journey.' He tells them 'everything starts in our imagination.' And so his ethereal approach to cuisine is intended to make the audience feel something special each time they visit.

EYAL SHANI - HASALON

The original world-famous baby cauliflower.

SERVES 2

1 medium-sized cauliflower
2 tsp olive oil
salt

Remove a small section from the base of the cauliflower, making sure the leaves are left intact. Bring a pan of very salty water to a rolling boil. Boil the cauliflower for about 7 minutes. It is ready when you are just able pierce it with a fork – it should still be a little firm. Take the cauliflower out of water and place on a baking tray. Let it chill.
Preheat the oven to 250 °C (480 °F). Once the cauliflower is chilled, rub thoroughly with olive oil and sprinkle with salt. Roast in the oven until beautifully golden brown.

TO PLATE

Drizzle with a little more olive oil and a pinch of salt. Be sure to enjoy the leaves.

SIGNATURE DISHES — 225

Kwok Keung Tung.

THE CHAIRMAN, HONG KONG (CN)

Kwok Keung Tung took the helm of The Chairman in 2008, the first Hong Kong restaurant to win the honour of The Best Restaurant in Asia. There, he turns age-old Cantonese culinary tradition into contemporary dishes bursting with flavours.

—— Kwok Keung Tung's famous flowery crab is inspired by a typical Cantonese dish made for him in the 1980s by an old chef. 'I could never forget its taste,' he says. 'When I opened my own restaurant, it came to my mind instantly. I have modified a few things, adding clam juice to the original recipe to strengthen the taste, and egg yolk to create a silky texture. It's a new take on my old-time favourite.' Despite these new twists, the chef likes to keep things simple. 'As Julia Child said, "You don't have to cook fancy or complicated masterpieces — just good food from fresh ingredients." Cooking is to enhance the natural flavours of the ingredients, not to mask them.'

At The Chairman, Tung aims to continue the legacy of the 2,000-year-old Cantonese cuisine, one of the eight culinary classical styles of China and perennially popular for its 'pure, clean freshness', using locally sourced ingredients, particularly fresh fish, shrimps and crab, as much as possible. 'I like to create dishes that make diners feel like they are visiting a welcoming Cantonese home where they are treated to some wonderful food they have never tried before — food they will remember the taste of for a long time,' says the chef, who was inspired by his mother's and grandmother's cooking skills, and later by the melting pot of cuisines he encountered as a student and apprentice chef in Australia.

Among the colleagues he admires are his friends Zaiyu Hasegawa of Den and Daniel Calvert of Sézanne in Tokyo, as well as chef Tetsuya Wakuda: 'I still remember the amazing texture and flavours of his slow-cooked ocean trout. It was then I realised that cooking could be an art. I was deeply inspired and determined to open my own restaurant that same year.'

Today his search for interesting, forgotten ingredients takes him on exploratory trips to villages in South China. 'The vast land of China is like a treasure box with unlimited surprises,' he says. One thing though: 'I am terrible with recipes,' admits Tung. 'I cook freestyle and every time it may be slightly different. I need other chefs at The Chairman to help record the recipes' details.'

KWOK KEUNG TUNG - THE CHAIRMAN

Steamed flower crab with Shaoxing rice wine and chicken fat.

SERVES 4 TO 6

FOR THE FLOWER CRAB

1 live flower crab or mud crab, 800g–1kg
1 small piece of ginger, sliced
1 spring onion, cut into 3cm lengths
4 pieces of chicken fat
200g flat rice noodles

FOR THE SAUCE

400g fresh clams
400ml 10–15-year-old Shaoxing (Hua Diao) wine
1½ egg yolks

Clean and separate the crab into pieces, and rinse well, carefully removing the yellow gills. Twist off its legs and claws. Crack the legs and claws with the back of a cleaver. Drain well and set aside.
Rinse the clams, then steam for 10 minutes on a tray. Extract the clam juice. Mix the clam juice with the Shaoxing wine.
Arrange the crab pieces on a plate in its original shape. Pour the clam juice and wine mix on top. Sprinkle ginger, scallion and chicken fat on top.
Start boiling water in a big wok. Once the water has come to a boil, place the plate of crab into the wok and steam for 6 minutes. Take the plate out, and remove and discard the ginger, chicken fat and spring onion.
Pour the wine and clam sauce into a separate bowl. Whisk in the egg yolk.
Pour the sauce mix back onto the crab, and steam for another 30 seconds. The crab juice will mix with the sauce and form a pool of golden liquid.
Steam the flat rice noodles in a separate plate for 5 minutes

TO PLATE

Add the noodles to the crab plate and let them soak up the sauce.

SIGNATURE DISHES — 229

Aaron Turner.

IGNI, GEELONG (AU)

One of Australia's most inventive chefs, Aaron Turner, trained at El Celler de Can Roca and Noma before opening the lauded Loam in Victoria in 2008. In 2012, he returned to his hometown of Melbourne to open Igni, where all food is cooked over live fire. His book Igni: *A Restaurant's First Year* made a big impression for its candid account of launching and running a leading restaurant.

— Turner's first restaurant, Loam, didn't have a menu, or even recipes; the chefs improvised dishes using the ingredients of the day. Thankfully for us, Turner's second Igni, which opened in 2017 in Melbourne's Geelong, does have some recipes, including his signature dish of fermented Dutch potatoes and smoked trout roe. It requires quite a few steps and involves fermenting ingredients for a couple of weeks.

But there's nothing truly complicated or overworked about it. 'My cooking is about simplicity: adding a light touch to ingredients using simple techniques to gain maximum texture and flavour without interfering with the integrity of the produce,' explains Turner, whose dishes 'let simple, often overlooked, ingredients shine.'

'I like to work simply and not over think things,' he continues. 'This relies on trusting and working with an excellent network of growers and producers in the area that I have worked with for 20 years to produce excellent quality-focused ingredients.'

Igni is an abbreviation of 'ignite' and the lighting of the fire Turner cooks by—a fire that disastrously filled the dining room with smoke on opening night. But it's been a success ever since, with standout dishes such as potato noodles cooked in chicken fat; slow-roasted quail; mackerel wrapped in Australian masa leaves; and oysters cooked in embers.

Despite his success, the chef remains completely honest about the hard work behind his culinary creations. 'I'm not sure passion is the right word to explain what I do; the hard work and long hours remove that,' he says. 'I think I am more intensely curious than anything, curious as to what makes a dish a dish, and curious as to what makes a guest experience the best it can be at Igni.'

Fermented Dutch potatoes poached in goats milk and single-press olive oil with smoked dried brook trout roe.

SERVES 6

FOR THE FERMENTED DUTCH POTATOES

6 large new season Dutch potatoes, peeled
250ml goats whey
100ml water
12g salt
200ml fresh goats milk
100ml first-press olive oil

Peel and wash the potatoes. Using a small melon baller, create the most perfectly formed potato balls you can. Wash under running water until the water runs clear. Keep the remaining potato for the sauce.
Combine the goats whey and salt and vacuum-seal along with the potato balls. Leave to ferment at 25 °C (77 °F) for two days, longer in the colder months.
Add the goats milk and olive oil to the fermented potato balls and cook at 90 °C (195 °F) for 1 hour. Chill rapidly.

FOR THE POTATO SAUCE

Repeat the same method with the remaining potato, leaving for 2 weeks to ferment, and cook at 100 °C (212 °F) for 1 hour. Blitz in a thermo until you achieve a consistent sauce.

Wash the roe in iced water.
Spray a non-reactive tray with a neutral oil. Add the roe and place above a fire so that it gently dehydrates from the smoke. This should take about 3 hours.
Season with the brook trout garum.

FOR THE BROOK TROUT ROE

100g brook trout roe
5ml brook trout garum

TO FINISH

20g smoked butter

Gently warm the potato balls in the sauce, adding the cold smoked butter to emulsify. Season with the brook trout roe.

Jorge Vallejo.

QUINTONIL, MEXICO CITY (MX)

Born in Mexico City, Jorge Vallejo trained at top restaurants around the world before coming back to his homeland and working at Pujol, where he met his wife and business partner, Alejandra Flores. Together, the couple opened Quintonil in 2012. A decade later, Vallejo has become one of the country's most influential chefs, known for his capacity to reflect on gastronomy and its respectful relationship with the environment and local communities.

x **What is your signature dish, and what is the story behind its creation?**

JORGE VALLEJO: *Charred avocado tartare with ant larvae and Mexican herb chips. It's the signature dish of the restaurant and my career, which I am very proud of. This dish showcases two of the most iconic ingredients of Mexican gastronomy. On the one hand, the insects - called 'escamoles' (ant larvae) - delicacies that have been part of Mexican culture throughout its history. You can easily find them at the local market, as well as in the most sophisticated fine-dining restaurants in the country. On the other hand, the avocado, a flagship ingredient of Mexican food culture. The fruit is very rich and flavourful, which makes it delicious to eat on its own or together with any traditional stew. It also has a lot of health benefits, with a great penetration of its nutritional properties in our bodies.*

Avocado is also too often stigmatised by foreigners as the « guacamole and chips », which has become a staple of «junk food» around the world.

My intention through this signature dish is to recreate for me « the perfect guacamole » mixing the particular flavors of the two identical ingredients to open the guests to another way to approach it.

x **How would you describe your cooking and the philosophy behind it?**

JORGE VALLEJO: *I think being a cook in Mexico is different from being a cook in other parts of the world, and I'm not talking about it being better or worse, just that in this territory we have a tradition of hundreds of years that is nourished by an immense amount of ingredients and recipes. In this sense, my cooking is an effort to express with my voice what I perceive, feel*

and understand in this vast universe. I do not so much seek to revolutionise or do something completely different; what I pursue is a style, a way of living the gastronomy and territory of Mexico, whether through memory, experimentation, research or observation. I hope whoever eats what I prepare will understand that through taste.

X **How and when did you become passionate about food?**

JORGE VALLEJO: *Since I was a child I have had an interest in cooking. In Mexico, passion is almost always born from our family meals, from our grandmothers, aunts and mothers in the kitchen. Almost unconsciously the family gathers in the kitchen, not in the living room. I could say that my career, from the beginning, is an attempt to revive and evoke this relationship of memory through taste, and being able to achieve it in the experience my restaurant offers.*

X **What are the characteristics of the dishes you like to cook?**

JORGE VALLEJO: *One of the fascinating things about cooking here is that you're never completely up to date, you are constantly learning. In Mexico, there are officially seven types of mole, but I assure you that if I visit some remote village in the middle of the Sierra Madre, they will serve me a unique mole that I have never tasted before, which takes completely different local ingredients, mixed with animal proteins - chicken or pork. The huge diversity of their composition inspires me constantly, and drives me back to my kitchen to do testings. I am constantly inspired by the richness of my country. The coastal gastronomy of Mexico for example has an immense food culture in terms of cooking with fish and shellfish. While the Yucatán peninsular has a very singular way of cooking, and so on...*

X **Does a dish have a calling? And if so, what is it?**

JORGE VALLEJO: *It's difficult to talk about a calling in something that doesn't refer to a person but if I dare, I would name the taco. The dish is multidimensional, adaptable and generous. It's eaten throughout the whole of of Mexico and has a culinary core that has nourished us for hundreds of years. It is nutritious, cheap and delicious. In Mexico it serves the poor and the rich, in the morning, afternoon, and at night.*

X **What is your best quality as a chef?**

JORGE VALLEJO: *Discipline... the mother of success.*

X **And what is your shortcoming?**

JORGE VALLEJO: *I'm a perfectionist, which on the one hand makes me better, but on the other hand I don't know when to stop. I doubt if what I am doing is right. Sometimes I have to stop, find the balance, and say that a dish is ready.*

X **Where do your main sources of inspiration come from?**

JORGE VALLEJO: *Family, traditions, the five senses.*

X **What is your main concern: originality or respect for tradition?**

JORGE VALLEJO: *As I already said, I'm not looking for originality as such, I even think it's an overrated term. For example, in Quintonil you will find tacos, mole and uchepos. None of that is new. What interests me more is the unique way I can offer those dishes, how can I address them through imagination, using different techniques, various presentations and combining different elements. This is how I design the menus, and in the end I want my cuisine to offer a journey through regions, ecosystems and communities in my country.*

JORGE VALLEJO - QUINTONIL

Charred avocado tartare with escamoles and Mexican herb chips.

SERVES 8

FOR THE SHERRY VINAIGRETTE

25g sherry vinegar
50g olive oil
2g salt

Put the vinegar and salt in a bowl. Beat with a balloon whisk and drizzle in the olive oil until the vinaigrette emulsifies.

FOR THE DRIED SORREL WITH BANANA VINEGAR (MEXICAN HERB CHIPS)

50g sorrel (picked leaves only)
25g banana vinegar

Pour the vinegar into a vacuum bag and add the sorrel leaves, seal and let stand for 3 hours until the vinegar has soaked into the leaves. Drain and spread the leaves across a wax-paper-lined baking sheet and bake at 100 °C (212 °F) for 1 hour with the fan on full.
Remove the leaves from the oven and let them cool until they become crunchy. If no fan is available, bake the leaves for 2 hours and then allow them to cool and become crunchy in the same way.

FOR THE BEURRE NOISETTE WITH CHILI AND GARLIC

125g butter
30g garlic sliced cut en brunoise (i.e. 3mm cubes)
30g onion sliced cut en brunoise
30g serrano chilli pepper, de-veined and seeded, sliced à la brunoise

In a saucepan, melt the butter over a medium heat until it reaches 135 °C (275 °F). Remove from the heat and allow to cool to room temperature. Once the impurities have settled, decant the liquid leaving the milky residue in the pan. Sauté the garlic, onion and chilli pepper in the clarified butter, taking care not to scorch the garlic. Remove from the heat and allow to solidify.

FOR THE ONION POWDER

6kg onions

Slice the onions finely and oven-bake at 300 °C (570 °F) for 30 minutes. Grind in a blender until the onion turns into a powder, then sift and store.

FOR THE SPINACH POWDER

1kg spinach

Place the spinach leaves on a baking sheet and leave in a dehydrator at 60 °C (140 °F) for 24 hours. Grind to a powder in a blender, then sift and store.

TO PLATE

TO PLATE

280g escamoles (ant larvae)
2 medium avocadoes
10g sherry vinaigrette
2 serrano chilli peppers sliced à la brunoise
10g onion sliced à la brunoise
5g chopped epazote
20g beurre noisette with chilli pepper and garlic
10g deep-fried kale (see note below)
10g dried sorrel with banana vinegar
50g onion powder
50g spinach powder
1 serrano chilli pepper, in rounds
1 spring onion, sliced into rings
zest of 1 lime
15g salt

Cut the avocado into 0.5-cm cubes. Place in a baking pan along with the onion. Scorch slightly using a blowtorch. In a frying pan, melt the butter with the chilli peppers and garlic and sauté the escamoles. Adjust the seasoning. Transfer the escamoles to the container with the avocado, add the chopped epazote, and mix everything together with the sherry vinaigrette. Dust the circumference of each plate with the powders, leaving the centre clear. Using a presentation ring, serve a portion of the avocado and escamoles tartare in the middle of each plate. Top off with fried kale, dried sorrel, onion rounds and serrano pepper rounds. Use a microplane to grate lime zest over the tartare.

NOTE: For the kale, discard the stalks and deep-fry the leaves in oil at 100 °C (212 °F). Remove, drain and sprinkle with a pinch of salt.

Poul Andrias Ziska.

KOKS, FAROE ISLANDS (DK)

Born and raised in the Faroe Islands, Poul Andrias Ziska has gone from trainee to head chef at Koks, where he aims to distil the taste and smell of the Faroese landscapes into adventurous contemporary dishes. One of the world's most remote gourmet destinations, the Michelin-starred restaurant has temporarily relocated to Greenland while they await the completion of a new home in the Faroe Islands.

× **What is your signature dish, and what does it tell us about you?**

POUL ANDRIAS ZISKA: *It's ræstur fisk and garnatálg, a dish that contains many key elements from Faroese food culture. First of all, there is the ræst process that relies on our special climatic environment, embedded in our island's history: in tough conditions and without the availability of preservatives like salt, we have developed this method of wind-dried fermentation to keep animal proteins. Secondly, the sauce is made from sheep's intestinal fat – the garnatálg – another very Faroese tradition, and something which embodies our commitment to zero-waste when we slaughter an animal. I added the leek ash and aged cheese. My cooking is about reclaiming some of the traditional Faroese flavours and modernising them sympathetically.*

× **What is the story behind its creation?**

POUL ANDRIAS ZISKA: *At Koks we try to bring Faroese element to the dishes, in a modern way. For example, I use cheese as an accompaniment to ræstur fisk. Although cheese is not a traditional Faroese ingredient, I use it to tone down the powerful raest notes and make them more palatable.*

× **Where do you come from?**

POUL ANDRIAS ZISKA: *I come from Tórshavn, the capital of the Faroes. The essence of my cooking is about fresh ingredients. We are never more than 5 km from the Atlantic Ocean on our islands and this means we can get what we need relatively easily and extremely quickly from harvest to plate. Vitality and elemental freshness are key to my cooking.*

× **How would you describe your cooking and the philosophy behind it?**

POUL ANDRIAS ZISKA: *In the Faroe Islands we have always eaten what is available locally, the plants, fish and animals that survive here. The flavours I create in the kitchen come directly from that landscape; they can be raw and powerful, and some of our ingredients, such as wild seabirds, may be challenging for our guests.*
Many dishes at KOKS also rely on the so-called fifth flavour — or umami — most obviously embodied in the ræst process. My dishes are very much about experimentation. While some recipes inherit the past, none of them are strictly traditional. Faroes has modernised very rapidly in the past decade, and winning our islands' first ever Michelin star and then a second (in 2019) was the recognition, I believe in a successful marriage between Faroese culture and contemporary high-cuisine.

× **How and when did you become passionate about food?**

POUL ANDRIAS ZISKA: *My love for food came gradually, and I always say I sort of fell into the restaurant world rather than having a long-term plan from an early age. I had a part-time job in a restaurant while I was still at school, and although I tried other jobs, it was the smells and excitement of the kitchens that instinctively appealed to me.*

× **What are your main sources of inspiration?**

POUL ANDRIAS ZISKA: *Naturally there are strong core influences — probably French and Japanese — but I am also interested in learning new techniques and experimenting. At Koks we don't want dishes that are over-prepared or dishes with too many ingredients on the plate at once. At the heart of it, the very strong tastes of my home islands were the most formative. Travelling is also always important for new ideas, and moving Koks to Greenland has been very inspiring. New ingredients and flavours got me excited when I opened 'pop-ups' in Singapore and Japan. The different terroirs and the dishes they produce are very important, and Greenland is one of the most challenging and unique places I could ever hope to experience.*

× **What are the characteristics of the dishes you like to cook?**

POUL ANDRIAS ZISKA: *I like a dish to have an identity, not too many competing ingredients or overpowering sauces, an essential freshness you might call femininity. Many of our dishes rely on ingredients that take a long time to prepare, but there are normally just one or two key flavours that come out when you taste the finished plate.*

× **What is your best quality as a chef?**

POUL ANDRIAS ZISKA: *That's hard for me to say. Perhaps my willingness to experiment and my calmness in the kitchen. The business of cooking high quality dishes is serious, and my chefs know what is expected of them. I don't believe in shouting or waving my arms about. Perhaps that's just how Faroese people are, we tend to be focused on the practical side of things and not get too emotional.*

× **What is your main concern: originality or respect for tradition?**

POUL ANDRIAS ZISKA: *You need both of these things; they feed off one another. But I think you can often pass on a tradition to the next generation by reinvigorating it with a slight twist. We see that process not just in cooking, but also in other arts. I think of the musician Annika Hoydal, who uses our traditional kvædi (Faroese ballads) but adapts them in contemporary folk settings.*

POUL ANDRIAS ZISKA - KOKS

Ræstan fisk and *garnatálg.*

SERVES 4 - 6

FOR THE POTATO PURÉE

90g cooked potatoes
9g butter
9ml cream
1.8g salt

Cook the potatoes and leave to steam off. Pass them through a potato ricer and mix in the butter, cream and salt while the potatoes are still warm.

FOR THE POTATO STICKS

2 potatoes

Peel and cut the potatoes on a meat slicer set at 10mm. Punch out the potato with a 10mm cutting ring. Save the offcuts for the potato purée. Blanch the potatoes for 45 seconds and cool in iced water, then store in an airtight container until needed. Allow approximately 15–20 pieces per person.

FOR THE GARNATÁLG DISCS

25g breadcrumbs
15g grated cheese
25g soft butter
25g garnatálg *(air-dried and fermented lamb's intestinal fat)*

Add the *garnatálg* to a saucepan and melt over a low heat, then turn up the heat and turn up the heat for 3 minutes. Now sieve the *garnatálg* to get rid of any meat crumbs, and leave to cool down to around 50 °C (120 °F). Add the breadcrumbs to a blender and blend into a flour-like appearance, then blend in the cheese to a uniform mixture and then the soft butter and *garnatálg*. Place the mixture between two sheets of parchment paper and roll out to an even 3mm layer and freeze. When frozen, use a 67mm cutting ring to punch out the cheese discs and store on parchment paper in the freezer until needed.

FOR THE RÆSTUR FISKUR

1 fillet of fermented ocean perch (approx. 200g)
500ml water
15g salt

Dissolve the salt in the water. Add the fillet to the brine and let it cure for 12 hours. Remove from the brine, pat dry and then roll up in a plastic wrap. Steam at 70 °C for about 25–35 minutes, depending on the thickness. Leave to cool, and then freeze the roll. Keep in the freezer until needed.

FOR THE LEEK ASH

1 leek

Cut the leek in half lengthwise and separate the layers. Cook in the oven at 300 °C for 30 minutes until completely burned. Blend the burned leeks into a fine powder.

FOR THE CHEESE BASE

70g mature cow's cheese
70g water

Cut the cheese into small pieces and add to a saucepan. Add the water and simmer for 20 minutes, stirring every now and then. Strain the cheese base and leave to cool. Store in an airtight container in the refrigerator.

FOR THE CHEESE SAUCE

80g cheese base
16g reduced cream (reduced by two-thirds)
8g butter
3g cornflour mix (1 part water, 1 part cornflour)
0.8g lecithin powder

Add the cheese base, reduced cream and butter to a saucepan and bring to the boil. Thicken the sauce with the cornflour mix and then blend in the lecithin with a hand blender.

TO PLATE

Warm the potato purée in a saucepan, transfer to a piping bag and then cover the bottom of a bowl with the purée. Place a *garnatálg* disc over the potato purée and char with a blowtorch. Place the potato sticks around the bowl and then sprinkle with leek ash. Warm the cheese sauce and foam with a hand blender. Grate a small amount of the frozen fermented fish over the dish at table-side and finish by pouring the sauce.

WEIGHTS

20g	¾ oz
25g	1 oz
40g	1½oz
50g	2oz
60g	2½oz
75g	3oz
100g	3½oz
125g	4oz
150g	5oz
175g	6oz
200g	7oz
225g	8oz
250g	9oz
300g	11oz
350g	12oz
400g	14oz
450g	1lb
500g	1lb 2oz
550g	1¼lb
600g	1lb 5oz
650g	1lb 7oz
700g	1lb 9oz
750g	1lb 11oz
800g	1¾lb
900g	2lb
1kg	2¼lb

LIQUID MEASURES

METRIC	IMPERIAL	US
25ml	1fl oz	
50ml	2fl oz	¼ cup
75ml	3fl oz	
100ml	3½fl oz	
120ml	4fl oz	½ cup
150ml	5fl oz	
175ml	6fl oz	¾ cup
200ml	7fl oz	
250ml	8fl oz	1 cup
300ml	10fl oz/½ pint	1¼ cups
400ml	14fl oz	
450ml	15fl oz	2 cups/1 pint
600ml	1 pint	2½ cups
750ml	1¼ pints	
900ml	1½ pints	
1 litre	1¾ pints	1 quart

PHOTO CREDITS

1 *Suzan Gabrijan* / 2 *Quintonil* / 11 *Alajmo* / 13 *Sergio Coimbra* / 15 *Andoni Epelde* / 18–19 *Erika Ede* / 21 *Sara Santos - Arzak* / 23 *Magdalena Staurino – Arzak* / 25 *@restaurantgaa* / 27 *@restaurantgaa* / 29 *Amélie Vincent* / 33 *Neolokal* / 35 *Mikel Ponce* / 36 *Mikel Ponce* / 40–41 *Mikel Ponce* / 43 *Luis Mileu* / 45 *Grupo José Avillez* / 47 *Grupo José Avillez* / 49 *Georgiy Kardava* / 51 *Twins Garden* / 53 *Callo Albanese & Sueo* / 55 *Paolo Terzi* / 57 *Amélie Vincent* / 58 *Helena Peixoto* / 61 *Rubens Kato* / 63 *Lido Vannucchi* / 65 *Giovanni Panarotto* / 67 *Joan Valera* / 69 *Francesc Guillamet* / 71 *Vea* / 73 *Vea* / 75 *André Chiang* / 77 *André Chiang* / 79 *Christopher Shintani* / 81 *Saison Hospitality* / 83 *Matteo Carassale* / 86–87 *José Luis López De Zubiría* / 89 *Stephanie Biteau* / 91 *Stephanie Biteau* / 93 *L'air du temps* / 95 *Amélie Vincent* / 96–97 *L'air du temps* / 99 *Amber* / 101 *Amber* / 103 *Yam'tcha* / 105 *Sanchez Hadrien Perrin* / 107 *Mikla* / 109 *Mikla* / 111 *Claes Bech-Poulsen* / 113 *Claes Bech-Poulsen* / 115 *Den* / 117 *Amélie Vincent* / 119 *Lennert Madou* / 121 *Sergio Herman Group* / 123 *Amélie Vincent* / 124 *Amélie Vincent* / 127 *Kristoffer Paulsen* / 129 *Brae* / 131 *Sorn* / 133 *Sorn* / 135 *Pieter D'Hoop* / 137 *Amélie Vincent* / 139 *Maureen Evans* / 142 *Laura Lajh* / 143 *Laura Lajh* / 145 *Aya Brackett* / 147 *Benu* / 149 *Aponiente* / 151 *Aponiente* / 153 *MUME Hospitality Group* / 154 *MUME Hospitality Group* / 157 *MUME Hospitality Group* / 159 *Amélie Vincent* / 161 *Central* / 163 *Central* / 165 *Diverxo* / 169 *Diverxo* / 171 *Marie-Louise Munkegaard* / 175 *Marie-Louise Munkegaard* / 177 *Peter Ash Lee* / 181 *Diane Kang* / 183 *Yohann Vorillon* / 185 *Fred Lahache* / 187 *Amélie Vincent* / 189 *Edoardo Pellicano* / 191 *Burnt Ends Hospitality Group* / 193 *Burnt Ends Hospitality Group* / 195 *Anne Emmanuelle Thion* / 197 *Flocons de Sel* / 199 *El Celler de Canroca* / 201 *El Celler de Canroca* / 203 *Projecto Matéria* / 205 *Projecto Matéria* / 207 *Odette Restaurant* / 209 *Odette Restaurant* / 213 *Suzan Gabrijan* / 215 *Suzan Gabrijan* / 219 *Prateek Sadhu* / 221 *Prateek Sadhu* / 223 *HaSalon* / 225 *HaSalon* / 227 *The Chairman Group* / 229 *Amélie Vincent* / 231 *Igni* / 233 *Igni* / 235 *Quintonil* / 238 *Quintonil* / 241 *Koks* / 244 *Koks*

www.lannoo.com

Sign up to our newsletter for updates on our latest publications on art, interior design, food & travel, photography and fashion, as well as exclusive offers and events.

CONCEPT
Amélie Vincent (@thefoodalist)

TEXTS
Léa Teuscher
Amélie Vincent

COPY EDITING
First Edition Translations
Melanie Shapiro

BOOK DESIGN
Katrien Van De Steene
(Whitespray)

COVER IMAGE
Parsnip and apple, signature dish
Dan Hunter (Brae), © Brae

If you have any questions or comments about the material in this book, please do not hesitate to contact our editorial team: art@lannoo.com

© Lannoo Publishers, Belgium, 2023
D/2023/45/6 - NUR: 440/500
ISBN 9789401488303

All rights reserved. No part of this publication may be reproduced or transmitted in any form or by any means, electronic or mechanical, including photocopy, recording or any other information storage and retrieval system, without prior permission in writing from the publisher.

Every effort has been made to trace copyright holders. If, however, you feel that you have inadvertently been overlooked, please contact the publishers.